Author photo by Paul Neads

Gerry Potter is an author, poet, playwright, actor and director. He is also both creator and destroyer of Chloe Poems, the infamous gay, Scouse, Socialist, gingham-clad, drag queen diva. Gerry trained at Liverpool's Everyman Youth Theatre and National Museums Liverpool lists him among the city's leading LGBTQIA+ icons. His autobiographical poetry-theatre show, *My Scouse Voice*, was performed by Fenella Fielding at Liverpool's Unity Theatre, and a portrait documentary film, *My Name is Gerry Potter*, premiered at Homotopia.

Gerry's poetry collection, *Planet Young*, was Bafta-winner Sophie Willan's chosen book on BBC TV's *Between the Covers*.

GERRY POTTER
6A Blackstock Gardens

Flapjack Press
flapjackpress.co.uk
Exploring the synergy between performance and the page

Published in 2023 by Flapjack Press
Salford, Gtr Manchester
🌐 flapjackpress.co.uk

f Flapjack Press · 𝕏 flapjackpress
▶ flapjackpress2520

ISBN 978-1-7396231-0-4

f Gerry Potter Poet · 𝕏 GerryPoetry
📷 GerryPotterPoet · ▶ Gerrypotterpoet

Cover art & design by Paul Neads
🌐 paulneads.co.uk

Printed by Imprint Digital
Exeter, Devon
🌐 digital.imprint.co.uk

A UNESCO City
of Literature

For Jelly Beans.

Introduction

There are things I don't and can't remember and there are things I will and can. Recall as a notion puzzles me in much the way time and placing time does. I know I was young; I know I was youthful and now I know I'm olding. Getting here has been quite the journey; much of that journeying about mine and others lives, their lives and deaths.

Born in 1962 means I'm clearly a child of the sixties, being only eight years old when that decade ended. The oddest thing is so many of my now active memories are of then, sometimes I wonder how they are, why that is. Of course, some of that is the rather pedestrian, just *remembering*; much of it stories that have always been told, passed down by family, visibly relished and reimagined by them. But it's the still profoundly felt emotional fervour of *why* they have to be remembered mattering. Every story grounded, embedded and buried in searingly life-lived truth.

I'm terribly fond of The Ship of Theseus myth/thought experiment. A ship extremely aged, damaged, and forever rebuilt, that one day it was so rebuilt not one of its original components existed. It was never recognised as a new ship though. However many times it was sunk and resurfaced, then manually reconfigured, it was only ever The Ship of Theseus. In a way, this galleon wasn't allowed to die. Thing is, the thing I wholly love, it wasn't even ever a gigantic wooden ship, just a decoratively spilled fireside fable. Now it's a definite story of a much-rebuilt galleon that never in fact existed. Just a philosophically passed down, passed on memory (a ghost ship before it ever lived). So then, do memories somehow, some way corporeally exist? My guess is a long thought through, even longer intellectually examined, *yes*. I don't say that with any spiritual or metaphysical knowledge, I haven't those belief systems. But I do believe in the solidity of memory, so therefore I have to believe in a tall ship that never was. As much as I am a child of the sixties, I'm also a child of the Mersey, and well-versed in tales of tall ships that never were.

6A Blackstock Gardens is a book of two halves. First half a whirl-winding maelstrom of Scouse actual, not Grecian mythical, remembrance. A tumbling litany of lengthy told, heart-nurtured familial tales and, of course, love. Love for my family, community, and the gigantic red brick tenement housing us all. Get yourself ready for robust, rough 'n' ready regalings of really long roads and chimneys. A literary, literal rogues gallery of the fondly recollected, of the putting-names-to (I adore names), of the clearly and foggily excavated, and of the once again recalled-to-mind. A shout-down-the-mountains goldrush yell of the all-but-gone (there be memories in them thar hills), shook through the sifting pan of language, searching for those earthy, long hidden, but still glistening nuggets. Well, these are Liverpudlian, Scottie Road, Vauxhall Road, Dock Road, golden nuggets, where dirtied tarnish is just as valuable (if not more valuable) as attracting shine.

This first half of the book, even though they may judder in the slipstreams, is written very much in a past tense. Tenses and where and why they might matter have been a tricky boat to sail in. Because memory and often the impacting vivacity of remembering is so kaleidoscopically blurring, even in the first half I find myself right back bang in the middle of whatever the situation. But eh, this is a book about remembering, honouring remembering, and a largely sixties Liverpool, so there's gonna be surreal hits of abstracting, contradicting tenses fondly landing in the moments of it all… pop art time travel.

I'm pretty sure I am mostly right about all I've written, if not about names, then certainly about situation. So, while we deffo daily-played Rush, her name might not have been Miss Purcell. Believe me, when writing a memoir, gaps 'n' cracks have to be filled. Autobiography is a crazy-paved path of time 'n' place mismatched continuity, communally walking along one of the three long 'n' winding roads I've already mentioned.

There's the odd person from those days still around. Our Janet's (my sister-in-law) still alive, so I could have asked her about actual events, but creatively decided everything had to be about how I remembered it. This is *my* story and something about it being only mine is how 'n' what I want it to be.

Fire has a way of transporting; you travel with 'n' within it, it brings you into the moment. So, certainly within and after the 'Bommy Night' chapter, those tenses, although still very much the past, become far more present-day feeling.

After writing the first half of the book, for my sanity's sake, I had to take a year away from it. At that time, I'd already spent near two years with a psychologist being treated for Complex Post-Traumatic Stress Disorder (a psychological condition largely about extended childhood trauma). The second half of the book is where my c-PTSD starts. Eventually, we tried a trauma memory recalling treatment called EMDR (eye movement desensitisation and reprocessing). A difficult therapy to undergo but also a mind-blowing series of revelations. Not only could I not face writing the second half of the book, much of my memories/experiences of the time I'd blocked out. EMDR gave me back some (by no means all) of those experiences. Thing is, when under this treatment, you're adult *now* speaking aloud your childhood *then* trauma, so it in some way conjoins you both. Adult me becoming as much me as childhood me made me my own Ship of Theseus. It was only then I could begin to start writing the second half of what becomes a much more much linear tale (most of it takes place in just four short months) as a present-tense-speaking old and young me. I hope that makes tense, er, I mean, sense.

All in all, it's taken just over three years to complete this book. I have to be honest, it's something I at first thought impossible to do. As much as I loved my early childhood in Blackstock Gardens (and I beyond adored it), remembering unimaginable tragedy emotionally takes it out of you. Writing it, bringing it back, more so. My immediate family are all gone now, so resurrecting them, whilst at times wildly joyous, has also been something of a flashbacking head-fuck. I couldn't have done it without the invaluable help of my dear friends Maria Barrett (I think I read her the whole damn book down the phone), Caleb Everett, proof reader Rod Tame, and Flapjack editor-in-chief, Paul Neads. Without their carefully constructed inputting and encouragement, it simply wouldn't/couldn't have happened.

Yes, I'm called Gerry Potter and my family are the Butlers, all I've done is change my name. But nothing can change where and who I'm from. As a Potter I'll always be an out 'n' proud Butler (I'm still a Buck, a Butch 'n' a Jelly Beans). What a family we once were and what a family we still are. I can tell you now, big life has never stopped happening to us. Memoir is stone-skimming hits on the surface of the sea; it's the sea housing the whole story. Ask The Ship of Theseus, it knows. This is just the skimming hits of eight years of that big life, those big lives.

Gerry Potter
August 2023

6A Blackstock Gardens

I
Blackstock Gardens

Its name might suggest something a little greener, but the immediate thing striking any visitor about where I was born would have been that there wasn't a single blade of grass or blossoming bud. Plenty of red bricks mind, millions of them, but definitely no fields or flowers. Unless of course you're creatively agile enough to think of red bricks as flowers. In that case, my three squared-off row of tenements were a bountifully clustered, flagrantly presented, trio of bouquets.

I'm a day-jobbing poet on the sly, so can, often do and on occasion have had to see red bricks as flowers; footy-playing peonies, car-robbing carnations, rough 'n' ready roses, pungently lippy lilies. As for their non-poetic scent... they fuckin' stank! Surrounded by fiery fumes of so much pollutant-belching industry meant these hard-arsed, curse-hardy blooms carried about them a sulphuric aroma of Hades. Oh, but warra hell, warra community, warra gutturally real/surreal sense of home and gardens.

Long demolished and forever romanced, these now legendary tenements were folk-spun stories eloquently woven by themselves. Those stretching rectangular blocks were main protagonists in many a well-thumbed, dog-eared, three 'n' sixpence novel of drunken back-alley, knee-trembling ribaldry. Originally slang'd *The Billogs* (Scouse for 'The Buildings'), they looked statuesquely amazing. Everybody, liking or not, port 'n' parcel of the same stumbled-along, Dock Road, star 'n' sawdust reverie.

Once heralded a utopian housing revolution, for a while and for a great many, they were. The largely slum-dwelling population of the time was dangerously overspilling, so late nineteen-twenties/early nineteen-thirties Liverpool became one of a few British cities taking on board ideas of massive, modernist multi-dwellings. The then Liverpool Corporation instructed their town planners, architects and engineers to visit Amsterdam, Vienna and Berlin, and had them clock the latest progressive housing developments in those rapidly expanding industrial landscapes. Of-the-moment architects such as Erich Mendelsohn were invited over to lecture/advise and those stylish European designs could be strongly seen/felt in the often Art Deco sculpting of the many tenements built.

Knee-high sat on my mother's lap, I'd intently listen as she'd tell of those horrific hovels. How, like so many, she all but escaped the worst of them and how the worst of them were a too-cramped, cockroach-infested, sewerage-stinking uninhabitable. These new five-high mega structures would be seen as up-to-the-minute luxury council housing, possessing two to four bedrooms, a decent-sized living room, separate kitchen, inside toilet/bathroom, inside coal hole, gas/electric lighting and huge, safe, recreational spaces for children. Escaping filthy, damp, vermin-riddled accommodation to be re-housed in one of these monolithic new apartment blocks was the life-changing/saving preoccupation of most working class Liverpudlian families. Maybe that's why, for all their surface gothic modernity, they were so cryptically florally christened. Compared to the crumbling, over-stuffed squalor they'd many-decades-endured, the finely-carved architectural brutalism of Ashfield, Gerard, Vauxhall, Hopwood, Thomas White, Woodstock, Fontenoy and Blackstock Gardens would have appeared a mountainous red brick Eden.

Oh, there were men, lots of them. Big, muddy-booted, still stubbornly Brylcreem-quiff'd, size of barn door men. Stomping, clomping about in dirty overalls men. What's for tea an' 'ave you ironed me fuckin' shirt yet men. Down the ale 'ouse, holding court, spouting dirty jokes, drinking fourteen pints of mild and knocking seven kindsa shite outta each other men. Putting on bets, losing on winners, song-singing, life-winging, making damn well sure you knew they were there still, ding-a-linging men. But those tenements were also full of big women boasting huge families, forearm-smashing a barnstorming way through the everyday onslaughts of everything that could possibly be thrown at them. Notions still nostalgically cradled are the split-second-spat hilarities of those turbo-charged women. Even too young to pick up the multi-layered gravitas of what they were guffawing about, their raucous cackling always felt like circled protection. Cigarette-mouthed, Vauxhall/Scottie Road broads, in super-quick time, twisted-tonguing a whiplash of perfectly punchlined jokes, bullseye-aimed at their hard-at-work blokes. Them holding a chipped cuppa cha in one hand, Sayers chocolate éclair in the other, uncontrollably howling at their fellas' all too real and hugely exaggerated inadequacies still cracks me up.

More than powdering, grey glues of cement and ruddy, emblematic size/scope of design, it was heightened interconnectivity of conversation holding those communities together. A near-humming, almost/always half-heard chunnering sound, communally engine-ing everything, everybody, everywhere; the far-too-busy, far-too-concerned narrator of their own and everyone else's jangle (Scouse for 'gossip'). Long before the World Wide Web began conjoining us, jangle was our local, furiously fast, ears-whispered, big-gobbed, loose-lipped internet. Believe me, if anything of conversational merit had just-this-minute-happened down the road it would take but a mere couple of seconds for everybody up the road to know all about it. Hearts may well have been stereotypically big but walls were paper-thin and, with a quizzically well-aimed ear jammed against them, everything could be heard. My earliest memories are made up of many things but, more than anything, it has to be the experientially linked, bubbling intensity of those deadly serious 'n' snidely giggled mutterings. There was always a juicy bit of jangle jingling away; somebody forever had something on someone.

Though all three gardens/squares/bouquets were a wide-shouldered dominant, like the sci-fi miraculous TARDIS in BBC TV's *Doctor Who*, everything was much bigger and far more fascinating on the inside. One of those TARDISes, 6A Blackstock Gardens, was a second-floor corner apartment of a five-storey building. There were two other flats alongside our landing and at the end, with a stairwell between, on a sudden right-angle, a whole other lane. Some opposite had even longer landings/lanes. Written down it reads a municipally-cluttered-compact and although in some ways was, it was also an airy, roomy, linear complex. Not quite so mind-tricky on the eye, but a lot like a council-built Escher print.

Nineteen-sixties Catholicism was a daily-bludgeoned, richly-coloured ubiquitous and weighty Bible passages common as early reading Ladybird Books, making me as at home with Satan as I was with Rumpelstiltskin. Being brought up on tales of heaven/hell and baby-stealing pixies made me think the Devil itself might be living/breathing a few feet under the bonfire scar of our front tarmacadam'd square. An oddly comforting thought. Well, I was a spooky kinda kid. The idea that any-second about-to-pounce demons 'n' ghouls lurked around every corner delightfully terrified the ghost-storied bejebers outta me. Being a predominantly Roman Catholic area (there may have been the odd Protestant lurking somewhere but, if were, they never said) meant hundreds of sugar-buttied-up, tatty-haired, Fenian tykes sped our hyperactive ways around those landings, zipping in 'n' out, up 'n' down, within 'n' about them like feral lightning. From our youthful perspective, with acres of running room and thousands of climbing possibilities, those lengthy thoroughfares were an exciting series of bold-stone mazes. Excellent for a quick game of hide 'n' seek or, as we called it, *hidey*.

One, two, three, four, five, six, seven, eight, nine, ten… comin' ready or not!

Mothers, grandmothers, aunties, sisters, again mostly women (lots of them religiously christened Mary, none of them virgins), would take hourly turns watching over the square, keeping a hyper-maternal eye on the twisting vortexes of children below. A series of baby-holding mothers, sometimes two babies, toddlers and a pram, looking out, making sure everything for every kid was safe. Jutting from those concrete sliding walls, appearing like tiny demon horns, were curved-hooked-ended, black metal poles. Tied to each was a nylon/string line, so each Scouse Madonna 'n' Child would be colourfully surrounded by the drying signatures of her family's just hand-scrubbed washing. Wildly billowing in strong Mersey breezes were dads' underpants, overalls, grandmothers' bloomers, brothers' jeans, school shorts, grey jumpers, Communion veils, terry towelling nappies, valance sheets, and the outré out-of-all-control Tiller Girl flamboyance of yer Ma's American tan tights… those blousy Music Hall washin' lines knew no shame.

A definite, parented-by-the-village ethos permeated everything and as kids we were readily welcomed into most homes. Certainly during the day, it was a *front door open, never closed* kind of community. You could lose count of the amount of cups of tea and pieces of toast you might have to get through. My favourite tea-'n'-toast-giver was the gorgeous Monica Jeffers, a fashionably vivid, perfume-scented young woman in possession of the shiniest black beehive and most startling blue eye shadow. Because I secretly wanted to wear it too, I'm now convinced it was Monica's electric-azure eye gloss that magically made me gay. Monica was as wholly confident as she boldly looked and, like most Scouse women, wittily brilliant at holding court. I'm pretty sure her younger sister Anne-Marie and I were toddler boyfriend/girlfriend, so for a while I was never out the Jeffers's. Those tenement flats had small, AGA-like, coal fireplaces/stoves, so, speared onto ordinary eating forks, bread was toasted over flames, slap-dashed buttered, curled around, then clumsily dunked into splashing tea. I'd stare transfixed, fascinated by the oily globs of Stork margarine left floating around the top of my cup. Looking like greasy planets, they'd ooze and coalesce about each other, tiny butter 'n' tannin infused galaxies; making me seem a junior yet wildly omni-present god. I also adored that three-sugared, lip-licking smell of stery-milk and the near-nose-dipping-in, hands-around-warmth of the mug, all of it smoothly twirling into the spiralling universalities of moment.

No sooner had we downed our tea 'n' toast, Anne-Marie Jeffers and I would bomb it out the front door, laughing out mad-dash chortles along the landing. Barely touching a step, we'd take a flying leap above the stairs, our shoulders repeatedly banging against stairwell walls, gleefully skipping into the rough 'n' tumbling spectacle of the world outside. Greeting us, belting out confidently sung sea-shanties, a huge ring of hand-in-hand girls spinning circles of rhythmically precise words, all calling out for future husbands, children or houses to live in. I was one of very few boys able to join in those games; yes, at five years of age, I was rhythmically circling and calling out for my future husband too. Tied around one ankle, some girls would have a cut-off leg of their Ma's nylon tights and, with a tennis ball stuffed at the other end, they'd twirl it around, hopping 'n' chanting as it speedily passed underfoot. On the ground, filled with the hurried infant scrawl of spidery white numbers, distorted chalk squares of hopscotch. Some clearly drawn that day, others ancient, weather-beaten, and long fading. Those scraggy hopscotch sketches were every-where, a scally-swaggering street-art; a pavement pre-Banksy Morse code only we could decipher. Then there was the seemingly endless joy of *Two-balls*: intricately executed ball games, repetitively battered against our red brick. Two-balls was the skirts-tucked-into-knickers, fast, furious, hand-catching of tennis balls. With goggle-eyed intensity, legs kicked high and bodies rhythmically dipping with over-arm/underarm pinpoint accuracy, looking to the world like an expertly juggling tenement-wise circus, there would be long lines of us wall-hurling revolving splats of brightly coloured sphere. Yes, it goes without saying, I also loved playing, and was fabulous at Two-balls. I loved it all, was intrinsically part of it all, and recall just how important the sea was to almost every rhyme sung. We were singing of tempestuous storms, sinking ships, drowned lost loves, tear-stained goodbyes to familial home-lands. It was a most poignant, hand-held, ball-copping, song-sung, romantically sea sick childhood.

Blag-Anne (aka Anne), Bunny (aka Mary) and Theresa, daughters of the bitingly comedic, always startlingly turned out, immaculately flame-coiffed Annie King, were my day/night-long babysitters. Their particular brand of babysitting was to take me to the top landing of their part of Blackstock Gardens. Above one of the square's gaping archways, they'd secure a docker's-arm-thick, sea-salt-stinking rope to some big, rusty metal hook. With noosed rope tightly tucked under arse, they'd then lurch from the last of the stairwell's four dark grey steps, swinging right out of that red brick portal into the welcoming glare of sunshine. No word of a lie, dresses tucked in, five floors up, they swung tall above it all, howling laughing as they rebelliously flew. Sat on those cold stone steps, heart pounding in my terrified gob, I'd be panicky-agog at their skilfully blasé bravery. Nothing was story-time passive or lullaby sleepy about being babysat in Blackstock Gardens.

Of course, the proper lads would be playing football, some-thing I'd vigorously eschew, but when it came to rounders and our versions of cricket or tennis, I was well in there. Being an expert and much-called-for slogger meant I could, with homemade cricket bat, slog one of those brightly-shaded balls for miles. Apart from occasionally smashing the odd window, we lost most of our balls over the roofs of far too many factories. Although macho sacrosanct, footy was set in football rules stone; everything else we played was *our* unique version of it. Even British Bulldog got the Blackstock Gardens makeover but we, being the collective individualists we were, called it *Rush*. The wonderful thing about Rush was anything/everything could be going on but soon as it was called, we immediately came together. Often it wasn't even called but like some psychic, prepubescent gestalt, we'd mystically find ourselves assembling to play. Rush was a game all kids could join in and on occasion, adults. We'd pick two to be *on* and the rest would diligently, backs against a wall, line up. I'm talking loads of us lined up here, then the two who were *on* and now some way away from us, would yell *RUSH!* Like a charge of bleating gazelle on a broken-glass, dog-shit strewn Serengeti, we'd hurl ourselves forward to get to the opposite side of the square. If caught or ticked (tagged) by any one of the two grabbers, we would automatically become grabbers too, until there were just two rushers and forty (or more) grabbers, making the last one rushing our glorious victor. Families watching from their lofty positions above would vocally join in, getting us to run faster. They'd be telling us to watch out because a grabber was catching up behind, using our nicknames and feigning four-lettered florid scorn if grabbed. Annie King would definitely have shouted, 'Fuckin' 'ell Jelly Beans, no wonder y'were caught, y'were runnin' like a bandy penguin there lad!' It was Annie christening me Jelly Beans; she was a most creatively prolific nicknamer. From six to sixty the whole of Blackstock Gardens played Rush. An uncontrolled, liberating noise emanated from that game, completely filling the square, an important a part of playing it as anything else. Thinking back, no one outside of our gang could possibly have understood what we were screaming. We weren't saying actual words;

whoops, jeers, hollers, whistles, off-kilter, high-jacked, banjaxed sounds were all the oral/aural communication needed. It wasn't just the pure joy of high-octane, limbs-knotted, blurring play; it was forty-plus kids everyday knowing each other and each other's families incredibly well. How wild communal trust sounds when you give it over to the instinctive feral intimacies and improvisational fervour of locked-in together children. There was a uniquely releasing music to that noise, a rebellious pre-punk choir, an anarchic, tribal-defining orchestration I don't think can ever be recreated… it was *our noise*.

After Rush we'd split into smaller gangs. I'd more often than not be with my nephews Little John and Stephen, who were only one/two years younger than me (I was an uncle aged one). I clearly recall Susan Graham, who because we shared the same 20th July birthday would call me her twin brother, and red-headed Gerard Campbell. Gerard was a bezzy (Scouse for 'best mate') and extremely popular with our gang because, living on the ground-floor, he had a swing in his yard. An actual proper playground swing, homemade by his dad. A daily beguiling swing we'd long queue up for and then climb over his wall get to. We could have just walked through their gate but we were scruffy kids, all about bruised knees 'n' scraped elbows; scratches 'n' scars our competitive flesh-torn currencies.

One night, slyly creeping out of 6A, I decided to mooch over for a nocturnal visit to the Campbells'. Because I adored where we lived so much, sneaking out, especially evenings or in darkness, was something I had to do. I needed to be alone around the enormously shadowing architecture; loved it overwhelming and dwarfing me. Feeling small 'n' lost in it all was always magically wondrous. Best lost I've ever been. I gingerly tiptoed towards the Campbells' wall, climbed up 'n' over and started secretly swinging. Oh, how I lived for those sweeping, dusk-rusting arcs of freedom. Factory smelly air, delicious hints of burning rubber tyres and the periodic dead flesh whiffs of our local tripe factory pungently rushed over my beaming face… close to flying as any tenement waif gets. Caught within the sensuous reek of it all and holding tight to cold, thick hoops of squealing metal, I swung higher 'n' higher. Every kid has their indestructible moments and this was deffo one of mine. I was a soaring mighty-hero invincible, Super Jelly Beans… but like all invincible kid-of-steel moments, about to cruelly encounter my Kryptonite. From high above, the tautness of the swing began to uncontrollably buckle. There was a momentary loss of control, a jagged, wobbling, criss-crossing of chain, resulting in me forcibly banging my chin on the top of its crossbar. Thankfully my tongue was on the right side of my teeth or I'd have lost it. A slightly concussed me came to and started screamingly crying. In a second and as if from nowhere a crowd of concerned adults were seeing to my every need. Feeling somewhat stunned and limp (fey being my go-to emotion), one of my brothers effortlessly carried me to our flat where me Ma promptly overcoat-swaddled me on the couch. With maternal, palm-to-forehead bluster and gulped down with a cup of heated-up cream soda, she hurriedly administered a couple of tiny pink Junior Disprin. Although near-death-mortally-wounded, I enjoyed being the busied-around eye-of-the-storm centre of it all. Until it was time to sneak out again.

So much manufacturing made where we lived a brilliant place to kick about in; not only were the local factories employing our families, they all produced something tangibly playful. On Blackstock Street itself we had a massive duck down warehouse, *the feathery* (it was and still is a Liverpool colloquialism to end almost everything with a *y* or an *ie*), so we regularly nicked goose feathers and duck down. We broad-daylight and under-noses stole lots of odd things from hosts of factories; giant cardboard boxes for makeshift dens, little see-through plastic beads looking like opaque hundreds 'n' thousands, or whatever was a fast-snatching grab 'n' quick getaway to snatch. We'd often get caught red-handed and be chased by older members of our own families, letting us know in no uncertain terms they'd break our fuckin' scrawny little necks when they got their hands on us.

There was a place called the BXL, possessing a huge, automated, corrugated-iron shutter; the kind operated by a tantalisingly nearby, shiny red button. Taking it in turns, one of us would creep into the kiln-hot heat of its workplace and press that more-than-inviting shiny red button whilst the rest hung onto its machine-chugging, slowly rising shutter. Tiny us, making something so massively, mechanically adult happen felt legs-kicking defiantly powerful, the finger-juddering surges of it delightfully thrilling. We loved it vigorously rattling our little bodies, making our giggling voices vibrationally warble 'n' squeak. And then, of course, deliberately swearing because *fuck* sounds even funnier when uncontrollably shaking. The game itself, simple: just who could hang on highest. But before our game could ever be successfully played, we'd be shooed off 'n' out by angrily shouting workers. Stutteringly yelling *SCRAM!*, we would drop to the ground and speedily scarper for our dear lives. We'll never know who could have hung on highest, because not one of us ever reached the dizzy heights of winning.

Industry crowded everywhere, with brightly shining factories hidden behind dark, auld Victorian/Edwardian façades. A bold palatial sense of style and design decorated most of our surrounding buildings. Being so near the city centre and a limp stone's throw from the Dock Road meant everything seemed perfectly placed and solidly there. Literally five minutes' walk from where we lived sprawled magnificently opulent dock-lands warehousing. The Waterloo Dock, one of the largest in the world, even boasted a little treasured island of its own. Proudly plonked in the middle of that island was a proper Giant of the Mersey, a five-sided clock tower known as The Dockers' Clock. Seriously, if any series of monuments were definitively storybook spectacular. These Tolkien-esque panoramas were where worldwide fables set a daily sail and we were everyday-used to that size of flagrantly told, merchant-seafaring storytelling. Vocally, Scousers are a sprightly breed, so adding that hacking, accented bravado to such picturesque vistas often felt like living in an illustrated, cuss-addled, docker's opera. From way back till this day, I was/am visually overwhelmed by the domineering masculine beauty of it all. I think it's safe to state that end of Liverpool was architecturally, phallically/ theatrically male. Saying that, it wasn't only men employed in those factories. Huge swathes of women were also the work-force. Tate & Lyle and The BA (British American Tobacco) had legions of female labourers marching to 'n' from employment; the million mothers of Vauxhall Road. There was so much labour, so many labourers, you'd be able to time your day by lines of shift-workers toing/froing from home to job and back again. It wasn't much of an enlivened vibe on a too-hungover Monday morning, but come Friday night those lines of workers were all but singing 'n' dancing, almost conga-ing home for the weekend.

At five o'clock on Friday, Blackstock Gardens felt like a more riotous version of Christmas Day than just another tenement. That many large families and so many men/women having just been brown-pay-packet paid was in itself a kind of party time. In the way squalling seagulls flock around boats to glide down on just-gutted, cast-off fish offal, young kids did much the same with returning from work mums/dads, aunties/ uncles, brothers/sisters. Pocket money day was wild! Here is how trickle-down economics should and does actually work. If you've a wad of just-earned overtime cash and you give a kid a tiny bit of that wad, then that pesky kid (along with a whole load of other pesky kids), by buying any amount of sweets/ crisps/comics, will with furiously shrill abandon pack out their local sweetshops, irritatingly harassing the increasingly short-tempered, ready-to-explode shopkeepers. A hysterically mad hour of those sticky-fingered silver shillings, thru'penny-bits and sixpences exchanging for chocolate goods and lemonade services was my kind of interactive capitalism. My sister-in-law, Mary Mac, worked in Marshall's paper shop on Vauxhall Road and absolutely loathed me scrabbling in on a Friday evening. Much later on, pissed-up in pubs, she would regale me with, 'Oh, y'were one fussy little shit you Gerrid (Scouse for Gerard), you'd 'ave me up 'n' down an' all over the place. Up that fuckin' ladder, down that fuckin' ladder, an' y'still wouldn't want what y'd just asked me for. Every time y'walked in, I'd raise me eyes to high 'eaven an' think *Jesus tonight 'n' tomorrer it's in, 'ere we go again...* tellin' y'now for nothin', y'were one bleedin' nuisance you lad!' Loved our Mary.

What was particularly brilliant on payday was 6A itself, because like most other flats it had in it the just-been-paid. Lots of those just-been-paid like three of my brothers, cockily young and wildly single. On Fridays, everyone seemed to have money and with that came a weekending confidence second to none. Before any of that partying and just after work, I'd be sent straight to the shop *on a message* by me Ma to get my brothers their particular brand of ciggies, a sachet of Vosene shampoo (always), a black plastic comb (sometimes) and *The Liverpool Echo* (obligatory).

Early Friday evening, my already half-bevvied siblings would charge in from town with bags full of new clothes, hit parade records, something for our Ma, and loads of delicious sweets for me. Then further rejoice by dandily trying on and cocksure prancing up 'n' down in their fab just-bought gear. My brothers' mates, pouring in with bottles/cans of ale, all cool-guy'd-up in their brand new clobber 'n' raucously readying for the night-time off, brought an instantly uplifting partying vibe with them. That sanguine assault of comedic celebration is what I thought being adult meant; gregariously happy giants relishing the moment, laughingly showing off, then just for the hell of it, laughingly showing off some more. Whatever was Number One in the pop charts (unless crap) was almost always played. I've definite, ecstatic, arms-in-air-elated memories of being thrown round our kitchen to Desmond Decker's 'The Israelites'. My brothers and their friends expressed such outward physical confidence; being flung everywhere was just what was done. Acrobatically hurled about any landing or street then somehow twirled up by the arms, bum-thumping onto their shoulders, was an everyday occurrence; an everyday occurrence zapped up to the max on Fridays/Saturdays. I was living with three much older brothers at the time, the jumping-up shapes of them, their slapsticking, pratfalling comedic ease, and just how much they trusted each other was everything to witness. I'd be in li'l kid brother heaven, blimping (Scouse for 'observing') their ever-changing shapes, real and shadowed. My brothers were often kaleidoscopic wall shadows and like rockin', rollin' storm-clouds, never the same jiving silhouettes twice. Enjoying their shadowing shapes meant double the number of brothers and us becoming a bigger familial gang. Even as a small child it was crystal clear to me something about this joyous weekending madness was about joining in and, just like Rush, clearly about being *part of*. Part of my brothers looking fantastic, knowing who they were, where they wanted to go and them easily able to get there.

Living so near the city centre they didn't have to go too far. When finally ready, or as they'd cockily exclaim, *dressed up to the knocker*, you should have seen how sartorially spot on they looked; expansive tenement red brick being the perfect runway-ing backdrop for such young buck sixties fashion. These sharp-suited blokes with hair newly quaffed and suited/booted, black-tie'd sleekness made their snazzy outlines jazzily shiver a seamless glide: the leathered muted glare and sheen-pointed shine of brand new shoes making their feet a just-polished ox-blood glow. The fellas of the square would often have wives and girlfriends alongside. I consider myself the luckiest gay alive because I'll go to my grave knowing I actually witnessed the full force of that decade's glamour. Women in just-below-

the-knee two-pieces, topped with the most impossibly constructed beehives… my sisters-in-law, our Janet and Mary Mac,
the heart 'n' soul of in-that-moment-bought boutique couture.
It seemed the weekend had special transformative powers
making our families magically change before our very eyes.
Adults always looked vitally important to me but their shop-
bought, off-the-rail glamour made them look like something
else completely – like Sharron Macready and Craig Stirling
from *The Champions*. I'd feel big, heart-pounding pangs of pride
in how they fashionably appeared, in my brothers and sisters-
in-law looking so groovily *with it*. Watching our Mary build her
beehive by her kitchen sink was a huge weekly buzz. I'd
deliberately inhale so's to catch the nostril-piercing smell of the
squeezy-bottled, thin-nozzled hair-lacquer she used. It would
hit my nose and back of throat like a tangy smack, and like a
smack it lingered for hours. There was a bright rhythmic uplift
to that creative weekending vibe completely about personal
reconstruction and elegantly poised presentation. They, with
high-styled, glamour'd ease, were confidently moving away
from the drab/oily overall/scarf of factory or dockyard floor
and into the Mersey-beating musical tremor of the night.

At night, and the way hungry puppies follow totally pissed-
off, full-teat'd bitches, we'd clumsily fall/plod behind our big
brothers/sisters, uncles/aunties, Mas/Das. We wanted to greedily
prod 'n' suckle on where they were going and what they might
be doing. There were two pubs either side of our tenement: Cons
(The Eagle) and Gerry's (The Feathers). First couple of pints
everybody would casually saunter to Cons, then, as it was only
a hundred feet closer to town, they'd pile in Gerry's before
heading toward the dancing neons of clubland. Everybody's
families were in those pubs and because of that I'd be hanging
outside with the Days', Campbells', Floods', Edwards' and
Murphys' kids; all of us sat on crates/bricks in the surrounding
waste ground, which we'd called *'ollers*. Taking it in turns, we'd
hang around the pub door then gingerly peep our heads inside

to ask if anyone from our families were in there. 'Is our John around?' I might say, knowing full well he was. 'I need to see him, cos something's just 'appened in the 'ouse an' me Ma's proper kickin' off.' Clearly well thought-through intellectual ruses getting Big John to come out with bags of smoky bacon crisps and a huge bottle of dandelion and burdock. We'd also get a good tellin' off for being up too late and told to get straight home. Other snazzy, dolled-up looking adults would be flowing in 'n' out the pub, so we'd be given and pocket any number of ha'pennies, pennies, thru'penny bits, tanners, silver shillings and (on a good night, depending how pissed they were) a whole half a crown. We'd have long built a small fire on our 'oller, drinking, chomping away and counting up our just-hustled booty.

Getting scant kid-glimpses into the adult worlds of those two pubs was an esoteric night-time's joy. Flock-wallpapered, wood-panelled, cigarette-smoky 'n' tawny raw, rhythmically pulsing with mesmerically dull-thudding, hypnotic sound. Defined by hacking roars of connecting laughter, those hazy celebratory visions crackled with howling delight. These were noises of people passionately communicating who they were, what they did or had that week made – and not only how they'd made said things but how they physically/emotionally felt about making them. There was a lot of union talk, a lot of politics, no end of dockers' jangle and tonnes of blue bawdy stories. This was a working class able to access the fashions and social mores of the time. Most importantly of all though, a financially buoyant working class, able to afford that all-important round. Seeing so many empty, half-full beer bottles and quarter-filled pint/half-pint glasses crowded on tiny spherical, battered copper-topped tables, would completely fascinate. I'd look to their muted colours and differing levels of ale; something about them shambolically collected together like that somehow reminding me of melody. Sensational sixties juke-box'd tunes would be silenced in a heartbeat if someone wanted to tell a big sprawling gag or ballsy balladeer a lovelorn lament. There'd be an accordion, banjo, guitar or piano player to hand and some full-throttle Scottie Road diva belting out 'I'll Take You Home Again, Kathleen', 'Sweet Sixteen' or, my favourite, 'Danny Boy'. As a six-year-old I didn't have the words but, within those precious door-peering seconds, I instinctively knew I was witnessing my culture. Family groups, their friends, effortlessly/eagerly entertaining each other, its homemade, handed-down, finely told histories being replayed, reformed and reaffirmed. This is what taverns in towns have always been. I was and still am a huge fan of vaudeville and thought that solely because of television (I'm a complete sucker for *The Three Stooges*), but it was *more* than telly. Weekly re-enacted in pubs, we had our own homegrown/homemade sense of vivid vaudevillian gusto. There was definitely an honouring *something* about being given the stage, the spotlight, and producing a more than confident performance. Even if sitting down singing, bodies would always turn to the singer, creating a pub-table-contained amphitheatre. Then, with out-loud audience appreciation of both singer and song, they'd be encouragingly cheered on like mad – *Go 'ed, Maureen girl! Gerrinthere Joey lad! Sheroo!* It was almost always the best singers who sang and more importantly, given the right space, the perfect mood to sing in. The North End of Liverpool, especially the slums and then tenements, were home to many of the city's Irish/Italian immigrant populations, and you could feel that singing/dancing, diaspora-infused influence everywhere. It was definitely alive and high-kicking every Friday/Saturday night, that's fer sure.

As we stood around our makeshift fire, devouring what was left of our crisps and gulping the last slugs of lemonade, we'd hear them calling from the landings. The choral night-wails of our mothers. Each one of us finely tuned into the ear-piercing sounds of our Mas' distinct yelling voices. *Y'd better get in now, an' I mean straight 'ome lad, this very minute if not sooner or there'll be murder!* Listen to them, Scouse Mas of the night, what music they make. Reluctantly, like the air surrounding had suddenly become densest treacle, saying busied goodbyes to each other and aiming to meet up and redo the same things tomorrow, we'd slow-wade our 'oller-draggin' feet home.

Before dead-weightily climbing the stairs to 6A Blackstock Gardens, I'd often take a precious minute to sit down and gaze up at its chimneys. Even they were showin' off how fab 'n' gear they looked. Sat, back against a late summer's daytime-heated red brick wall, it would radiate such relaxing warmth that, a soothed, cosy alone, I'd leisurely stare up 'n' across. Being so near the sea, the River Mersey threw up some of the most startlingly confident, late summer skies. Dramatically sprawled across the tops of our tenement, appearing like an amazing Cinemascopic light-show, coalesced huge, scarlet, deep purpling black/blue filmic gashes. It all looked operatically storm-scarred and tragic-theatre on itself; a bit *La Boheme* meets *King Lear* meets *The Ten Commandments* meets *The High Chaparral* meets *The Billlogs*. Silhouetted against that gorgeously showy God-painted sky, seeming stoically patrician, were our tall Blackstock Gardens chimney stacks. They stood wide-shouldered erect; bold, noble centurions, silent sentinels, mythically shadowed guardians, staring down and loyally protecting. These coal fire fuelled, smoke-belching terracotta legionnaires, like our banshee-screeching mothers below, deffo had a sword/ shield armoured eye out for us.

People often ask me my historic/present poetic influences. I usually witter out some people's names and can give clear thought-through reasons why I genuinely dig them. Having just written this though, I'm now convinced my first poetic influences were dramatic dockland skies and the perfectly distanced chimneys of Blackstock Gardens.

II
That Night

Lots of kids would have gone to sleep at a sensible time; Mary Mac putting nephews John 'n' Stephen to bobos by seven. My babysitters, the Kings, never hitting the sack when they should, I never went to bed early and not the only kid round our way doing that. We were a chosen few, a gang able to stay out that bit later and hang around the dying, spitting embers of our 'oller fire just a little bit longer. Hanging out around Blackstock Gardens till as late as we could was all we wanted, indeed, needed to do. We kinda knew we were kids who didn't kip when other kids did. It was just a thing.

Me Ma, May Butler, had already been well 'n' truly battered by what life could throw and needed me for night-time's companionship. Even then, before everything else, I was as much emotional crutch as youngest son. Not complaining here, completely loved being that crutch; it meant watching proper grown-up telly with her. Of course, I still more than adored afternoon, early evening kids TV like *Batman*, *Captain Scarlet*, *Thunderbirds*, *Joe 90* and *Land of the Giants*. I would eagerly edge-of-seat view then immediately re-enact them with everybody in the square. In particular, we loved playing Captain Scarlet. Gerard Campbell had the Captain's hat toy which, with a vigorous nod of the noggin, let the headpiece microphone drop to his mouth. Just like with his playground swing, we'd queue up to have a go. It seemed we were always queuing up for the Campbells. He even had the Captain Scarlet full body uniform and ray-gun. Gerard Campbell had the best toys. I'd insist on being evil Captain Black, the moodily still, sinisterly camp Mysteron (told you I was spooky). At night though, it was darker televisual territory. Flickering, monochromatic shows like *Danger Man*, *The Baron*, *Man in a Suitcase*, *Department S* and my favourite of all, *The Avengers*. The huge orchestrated blast of those first few bars of Steed 'n' Emma's theme tune instantly grabbed my wanting-to-be-grabbed soul. That conga-driven, stripper-burlesque-esque staccato immediately transported me from Scottie Road to espionage-riddled, posh London mews and the impossibly deadly, over-the-top dastardly insanities of evil masterminds. Next, the ears welcoming horns and the imagination caressing sensuality of its main melody, with me romantically rising and falling into every nuanced wave of its perfectly pitched execution. It's amazing the senses-tingling effect a jazzy minute-and-a-half of musical exotica can have on a seven-year-old, where/how it takes and reshapes you. Reshaping being the operative word; Mrs Peel was the first person other than myself I ever wanted to be and, if honest, still want to be... like Steed, every week I needed her. Although goggle-eyed with viewer exhilaration, there was still something eiderdown/antimacassar cosy about being sat behind y'Ma, near a roaring coal fire, playing with her frayed pinny-strings, watching surreally kinky, cat-like, leather-clad telly that was in-the-moment, mother/son perfection. No crazy, world-domineering, mind-controlling, people-shrinking diabolicals were ever gonna get their maniacal Cybernaut claws on me. Diana Rigg made being sat at the back of my mother on our favourite chair the safest place in the world.

The lads would be out in town giving it pure Liverpool laldi (Scouse for 'confidently drunken *whoosh*'), so for what seemed like ages it was just me 'n' May. Our living room, which we called the kitchen, was small and all year round felt a paint-peeling, nicotine-stained autumnal. We weren't a fancily fussy family. Well, except for above our chair, where we hung a beautifully painted, glass-framed Sacred Heart of Jesus. Catholicism's all about biblical familial trinities, so in a way Jesus was the third member of mine and May's private little gang. I profoundly loved Jesus, was never guilt-riddled or put off him for being all-powerful, never thought him a finger-pointing chastising, or omnipotently overseeing my every poo. May nightly-story-reassured he was our kind, knowing, celestial friend – so much so, I'd sneakily look to his glass frame and we'd secretly, telepathically communicate. Jesus could read minds and was a famed/framed listener; the best. Isn't that the whole point of prayer? Even now, in the wee small hours and as a decades-practised atheist, I often find Jesus 'n' I sharing the odd mind-jangle. Small, blue/pink, flowery-patterned wallpaper dressed the walls and a grubby, gravy-stained, purple curtain separated the kitchen from the back-kitchen (Scouse for 'actual kitchen'). 6A's evident sparseness was of no concern to my family. We'd historically few possessions so didn't much value them. Whatever sporadic pieces of ornamentation we may have garnered would have been Christmas/birthday-bought for me Ma by our Mary or Janet. Definitely home though, and in its own essentially bare way, aesthetically reflecting who we were and what we were about.

It might have been *The Saint*; May was in a lusty armchair love affair with Roger Moore and had been since *Ivanhoe*. She'd immediately, visibly physically bloat when he'd appear on screen, like she wanted him to see her at her womanly fulsome best, as if from the telly he could actually see her at her womanly fulsome best. There she was, suddenly spine-straight, smiling like a nymphomaniacal auburn-haired Joan Sims, almost as if getting sexually ready for him. All that was missing was a fetching, off-the-shoulder, blush pink nylon negligee. So, either *The Saint* or another firm telly favourite, *The Untouchables*, would have been on when, from outside, we heard my brothers' pissed-up stumblings-in from town. A just be-haloed Simon

Templar or machine-gun flashings of Eliot Ness could often accompany the joke-telling, jeering bluster of drunken brothers. For me 'n' me Ma it was never an ominous noise, just Friday/Saturday night normal. We were used to overhearing all kinds of inebriate singing or echoing arguing coming in from the landings. Didn't matter you were hearing fifteen different tunes sung by fifteen different singers; the more the pissed merry sang, the merrier pissed it sounded. Especially when aided by the natural reverb of those long municipal corridors, our neighbours over-emotive yodelling could warble an almost heavenly choral. Unless dangerously problematic or someone was clearly in trouble or door banging ubiquity of police, no one batted an eyelid or raised an eyebrow.

Something was seriously odd about this approaching noise though. Drunken as it ever was, but this time far more hurried and stressed, May immediately latched onto its bitty, heightened fractiousness. It seemed to be taking them much longer to get their key into the door. We could hear the rasping metallic scratchings of it missing the lock; sharp, scraping and desperate. With panicking chaos and arms-around-shoulders-carrying the limp body of one of their mates, my brothers all but fell into our hallway. They were drunk as they'd ever been, and I'd many times seen them at their worst, but this time far more unco-ordinated and jumbled. They were trying to hold up their continually falling friend, his lolloping side-to-side head chin-down on his chest, his dragging-behind-him legs clearly not working. Many a time they'd found themselves in fights (they were scally Scouse scrappers), so them piling in bruised 'n' bloodied was never a shock. What seriously rocked me was how erratically behaved they were. They looked uncharacteristically messy, seeming hopeless and unable, not really knowing what to do. They didn't look anything like themselves, their wall shadows clumsily shapeless; no skilled silhouetting acrobatics, just a hopeless crowd of thumping black. Sounds being made weren't organically connecting either, the exact opposite of their pre-going-out table-tennis banter; the same banter I'd recently seen them have with their clearly injured pal. There was high-pitched accusation, pushing temper, frayed despair and, punctuating it all, swear-studded jabbing yelps. What I was witnessing was brand new. I'd never seen my brothers this agitated or afraid. It scared me and I didn't like it.

Instantly taking control and effortlessly pushing them aside so she could properly tend to him, May instructed my brothers to sit their mate on our couch. With his head now carefully cushioned, my mother gently turned it to one side; from his right ear, a tiny trickle of blood. May's face instantly drew back, her voice commandingly authoritative, the only voice in the room: 'Get him to the hospital now!' It was all so madly busy, ruffled and cacophonous. I'm not sure whether my brothers somehow took him by taxi or there was an ambulance.

What I distinctly recall, after all that insanely physical, passionately emotive, vocally explosive commotion, was it being so quickly over. They just seemed to all-of-a-sudden disappear. I felt instantly left behind and dizzily disoriented, with only my agonised mother for company. She was quiet. Everything was quiet. A bizarrely intrusive quiet, the quiet you don't want, the quiet turning small spaces into vast deserts. In the midst of this overwhelming silence, I suddenly realised I was just a little kid and something massively adult had happened; something aggressively eventful and too much for me to fully comprehend. I was an unable to piece it together, spinning with it all, the only tangible thing the floor I was kneeling on. Our kitchen dank with an atmosphere I'd never experienced; bleak, weighty, and emanating from May. Sat at the very edge of her chair, she seemed in some sort of shock. As usual I did my job and dutifully climbed behind her. Rocking gently backwards, forwards, one hand clutching her elbow and her other thumb-thumping her lips, she said, 'That's not right that Gerrid. Oh God no, that poor lad, that poor lad.' The spread of my arms arced the width of her pink-cardiganed back and, with cheek on soft cloth of shoulder, I rocked with her. I looked across the room to see Eliot Ness still dodging machine-gunning bullets. Throughout all this muddied silence the telly was still on.

Not too sure exactly when, but let's say morning of the next day, we found out he'd died. Whether he died in 6A or hospital I don't know, but my mother knew something. She always did. There had been a massive fight inside/outside a pub/club and he'd been knocked unconscious. With it being just a saloon-type bar brawl, my brothers must have thought he'd eventually come to. He didn't. He was young and died.

That's when I first felt it, the clawing horror of grief; how physically/mentally debilitating it could be. For a long while there was a difficult-to-manage hush in 6A Blackstock Gardens, a heavy stillness coming from my brothers, but more so my mother. Nobody talked much; a lot of heads in hands, angrily slammed doors, and the laughter stopped.

It was to pick up again. Life always does. There were pay-days and pocket money to be had. But I'd soon hear that silence again.

III
May Butler

May would often delight in telling me, 'No wonder y'love bein' on that stage lad, y'was born to a round of applause.'

This is true and of course lovely, but the circumstances surrounding that applause weren't the best. Four months before I was born, May's husband, my dad Jimmy Butler, upped 'n' left her for another woman. This broke my mother into pieces, leaving her uncontrollably bereft. They'd never had the happiest marriage; my brothers telling me they were forever arguing and bickering. It's safe to say me Ma wasn't the shyest of arguers – the exact opposite being true. When it came to fighting her corner, and like most women round our way, she'd not only stand her ground but then hurl at you the pieces of pavement her stamping feet had deliberately cracked open to do just that. May Butler was a prodigious hurler. My dad was a much quieter person who'd only argue back if pushed but, as well as being a prodigious hurler, May Butler was also a more than accomplished pusher. A final separation was always on the cards, but when and after a few false starts he did finally leave, it devastated, almost killing her. She called it *pining like a dyin' dog* and hoped to God I would never experience anything like it: 'An 'orrible feelin' Gerrid, like someone's constantly rippin' y'insides out!'

May had lost so much weight, people who didn't know had no idea she was eight months pregnant, becoming quite a worry for family and friends. My mother couldn't eat anything because nothing would stay down, her nerves and psyche irreparably shattered by Jimmy Butler's sudden abandonment. She told me she always loved him, he was the only man for her that she was, as Judy Garland sang, *a one man woman*. It wasn't just the dimly lit torchings of love songs scarring 'n' scorching her. They were culturally embedded Catholics and way back then Catholics didn't leave or, perish the thought, ever divorce. In those days, not unlike swans, Catholics mated for life and, not unlike swans, one of them was often left circling the cold evening lake alone. My mother was old school religious, so there was still a mortifying shame if a marriage died and the bulk of that guilt/shame always carried by women. May completely took that on board, feeling like she'd failed herself, husband, family and God. Saying that though, it didn't stop her uttering on repeat the first phrase I consciously remember. I must have been a baby being winded over her shoulder, her hand patting my back to burp me, when first happening across its dulcet caress… 'Gerrid, y'dad's nottin' but a dirty, rotten, filthy, stinkin' whore-master.' Genuinely, they're the first strung together words I ever knew. From the womb and long after, being the recipient of such emotively composed Rabelaisian descriptors, it's no wonder I'm the kind of poet I am.

Near my birth there were talks of getting May to hospital, but for deeply personal reasons she wanted to have me in 6A. If my mother was one thing above anything else, it was immovably stubborn. Eventually, a sickly May fell into labour and I guess I was always gonna be as stubborn as she. My mother was a wailing 'n' ailing forty-two years old and I wasn't being easy on her. There were some complications, meaning May had three days/three nights of agonising labour. This was of huge concern to the community of Blackstock Gardens, so, along with the nun midwife, family and friends took it in turns to daily/nightly help. News had got around that May was nearly there and our little flat became full of worried women eagerly awaiting the moment.

For some reason, and the main one being it had to be a saint's name, I was originally to be called Anthony; a name she and Jimmy Butler had chosen together. In May's own words, the child-birthing screams coming from her were *unmerciful*. So, in a concerned gesture of Catholic healing, with beaded rosary in thumbing fingers, her close friend Maggie Mannon knelt beside her screaming head and started praying out loud to her favourite saint, St. Gerard. Soon as Maggie mentioned his sacred name, I popped out and a more than delighted midwife sister, lifting me to my mother's breast said, 'At long last May, here he is, little Gerard.' Within the first few seconds of my newborn heartbeats and brand spanking new Christian name, the collected women spontaneously burst into cheering applause.

Although sometimes operatically dining out on this story, that applause wasn't for me, it was for May Butler; it being instant, concerned relief that she and I were finally okay. Catholic, working-class women having lots of children, many born before the advent of the NHS, were no strangers to the horrific defeats of infant mortality. This time though, they were also communally worried about their Blackstock Gardens mate's adult mortality. An *other* sense of bonding rang all around that female Catholicism malarkey; of something not just about righteous religion, compliant guilt, Saturday confession, Sunday Mass or weighty biblical teaching. It was never just regurgitated catechisms 'n' fondly recalling fetching thirties/forties kiss curls; something psychically silent was woven all the way through them. They knew each other so well, it feeling headscarf mystic in its instinctive intensity. Along with the last war (and not just the last war, add to that The Depression), they'd shared so many similar experiences. Every one of them identifiably different, characterfully vivid, full of scars 'n' secrets. All remarkably individual, but something about/within/around them was the same. They looked at and read each other like books and I'm pretty sure it wasn't *The Bible*. When we talk of faith in purely religious terms, I think we sometimes miss the point. This energy, although clearly spurred and engined by religion, was far more than just church. It was dense, hard forged/fought for, shared experiential trust. I guess we call it faith because it's a lot easier to say than dense, hard forged/fought for, shared experiential trust. Even though at the time my mother was heartbroken and ill, whenever regaled by this story she was full of the most glowing kinship for those women. Her tearing-up eyes not for a recently disappeared Jimmy Butler or an agonising, arduously problematic birth but for her neighbouring comrades. She would oft' recall her Blackstock Gardens sisterhood with enormous fondness. 'They were great girls them Gerrid, great girls.'

When Jimmy Butler went, he left us without anything. All May had to bring up five sons with was a paltry cleaner's wage. At this point in our lives, we would have been what's now termed *underclass*, so thank God it was the nineteen-sixties and we then didn't feel the divisive need to invent such societally distancing labels. There were times we had absolutely nothing in that flat; no coal, no food, not even a silver shilling for the telly or leccy (Scouse for 'electricity') meters. In those despairing, candle-lit moments, everything seemed a hollowed-out empty. Like grief, that kind of poverty has a sound and like grief it possesses a most complicating quiet. A whispering flame around a sparking powder keg kind of quiet. A no man's land of breaking dawn before hearing the bombs go off and never knowing when those explosions would reach you kind of quiet. A lit matches between your toes and gingerly tippy-toeing over a jagged pathway of bangers 'n' rip-raps kind of quiet. At four/five years of age, it wasn't a soothing/comforting sound to experience. It certainly didn't relax, the exact opposite in fact. A quiet as far away from today's meditatively angelic mindfulness as it is possible to get. It was the sound of a lying-in-wait, raging, deadly assassin kind of quiet, and May could sometimes make those beady-eyed, skulking in the pampas grass kinds of noises.

I was about five years old so a foggy memory, but I must have taken it on myself to do something about one of our many foodless predicaments. One landing below we had the loveliest of neighbours, Mrs Dreah. Reminding me of Edith Piaf, Mrs Dreah was a dark-clothed, crucifix-wearing, slight woman who always had time for my mother. We couldn't walk past her door without her dragging us in for a session of tea 'n' toast (or in my case, a biscuit). Mrs Dreah was genuinely fond of me and a regular thru'penny bit and boiled sweet giver; a kid doesn't forget that.

One day, I snuck out of our flat, down two short flights of stairs, walked to her part of the landing, knocked on the door and said something like, 'Hello Mrs Dreah, me Ma's got no food in, 'ave you got any?' A concerned Mrs Dreah then brought me in and started rummaging around her larder. She took out a bag of potatoes saying, 'That's all I've got Gerrid, hope it'll do.' Thrilled by my cunning plan's instant success and with just-begged spuds in hand, I triumphantly headed back home. Once there, I immediately handed the potatoes to May. She suspiciously looked at them, then at me. With growing trepidation, I watched her eyes narrow scarily. She was getting incredibly angry and I could clearly see her four-foot-ten frame quickly become a tank. In a voice wretched with accusation, she rasped, 'Where d'you get these from lad?' Not quite the reaction I was expecting and I could only have replied *Mrs Dreah*. May immediately blew her top. She was never one to hide her feelings, but this time she went totally ballistic: 'Y'what, y'what, y'went downstairs and asked poor Mrs Dreah for spuds? She's got fuck all herself!' Again, I could only have said *yes*. Well, I got belted around the room, chased, smacked and, how me Ma would say, reefed (Scouse for 'being picked up by the ears and violently shaken'). Like every kid I'd get the occasional smack, but here she completely lost it like I had never experienced before or ever would again. She was bone-juddering raging, completely ashamed, then in a physically-crumbling second, uncontrollably weeping. After she had finished repeatedly whupping my toddler ass I went over to console her. Elbow on the arm of her chair, head in hand and big-breath gulping, she said, 'I'm sorry lad, I'm really sorry, I didn't mean that. God help us, oh God help us.' And she didn't mean that; it was one too many straws, the one breaking. That night we had chips.

Without a husband or any financial support whatsoever, and like many women, my mother had no idea about the then benefits system and so struggled bringing us up. She called them her *dark days*, telling me of the time she had to take all of us with her to pick up a parish food parcel.

Thing is, it wasn't at our local parish of either St. Brigid's or Our Lady's, but somewhere miles and miles away. Without money for bus fare and too proud to ask, she took me in her arms and, with the lads trailing behind, walked to this far-distant church. What would have really upset her was that it was winter, snowing, and my brothers didn't have proper shoes. She said a couple of them had something shoe-like covering their feet, but without any souls and were clearly just flopping about in the snow. 'Gerrid,' she would later tell me, 'I felt completely mortified. Anyone lookin' down could clock they weren't wearin' proper footwear. We musta looked like a family of tramps.' It was the bleakest time for her but she would always end the story with, 'Well, at least we had somethin' on the table that night, so worth it in the end, lad.' I know it sounds an over-melodramatic monochromatic, but May was a Scouser, so told it to me like a scene from D.W. Griffith's silent noir classic *Orphans of the Storm*. I recall hearing that story once as a kid, being quite put out that I was being carried in her arms and didn't have an actual pram. May's prompt retort: 'Shurrup will ye, soft lad, we could barely afford ciggies back then never mind prams! Who'd y'think you were, Little Lord Fauntleroy?!'

By the time I was born May had already lost two children. Her first had been Vincent who, when four years old, fell down a mere three steps. Such were the severity of his head injuries he didn't survive. Of the two, it was the death of my mother's only daughter Joan which upset her more. May seriously didn't want another son; she'd had six lads up until this particular pregnancy and ferociously hoped she'd finally strike lucky and at long last bag herself a girl. Back then, rules were so firmly the rules, that daughters were a necessary lifeline for struggling mothers. Annie King and her daughters were an arms-folded, shoulder-to-shoulder, close-knit pack. May semi-enviously noticed that and longed for exactly the same, saying, 'Gerrid, those girls don't bring an ounce of trouble to Annie's door, not like my lads.' It was a difficult pregnancy, with our Joan being born two months premature and May in such pain that she had to be hospitalised. Because of the trauma and painkilling medication she could recollect only phasing strobing moments, stuttering this story in on/off filmic flashes. She knew she had never been in such discomfort and that *somehow* a baby girl had been born, but in between that echoing agony and joy she had no real idea what was happening. Aware it was at last her precious girl, everything else seemed chaotically unimportant. The only things holding anything together, her desperate panic and maternal need to simply cradle her daughter. All she clearly remembered was her arms outstretched, reaching to hold Joan, and the doctors/nurses hurriedly taking her baby girl away. She'd recall a thick, bloodied, shock of jet-black hair and her child's wailing, telling me she'd never heard a baby cry so loud: 'As they took her away from me, I just saw her get smaller an' smaller Gerrid. Didn't even get to see her face.' Our Joan being raced down a long hospital corridor was the first and last time May laid eyes on her. After that, my mother swore if she ever got pregnant, she would never again have her baby in hospital.

May shared lots of fairy stories, she was great like that, but she'd regularly tell me of Vincent and Joan. Along with tales of Hansel and Gretel, I was also knee-weaned on stories of my dead brother and sister. I know she was sadder about her daughter than son because I'd hold May tighter when she talked of her. Such the tangible, storytelling lament of her voice, our Joan would always be my sister. I never grew up with Vincent as a sibling notion but did with Joan. She only had fourteen hours on this earth but I still have a sense of my sister today, with me now. May would also take time to stress, throughout all that horror Jimmy Butler was her lifeline, telling me he handled everything and her brilliantly. She couldn't have got through it at the time or afterwards healed without him. One of the few times she'd fondly talk of him and he wasn't a dirty, rotten, filthy, stinkin' whore-master.

For a four-year-old, finding your mother shaking and panicking at the front door is the strangest sight. I neither have a time nor date, but the startling visual has never left me. Someone must have knocked-on and my guess is May went to answer and froze. I'd seen/heard her scream, shout, cry, whisper and laugh many times before, but I'd never seen/heard her uncontrollably jibber. Such the pathetically withering noise coming from her mouth, it didn't sound like her at all. She was clearly unable, lost, and didn't know what to do. Only thing I knew was it was a frightened noise and she was obviously terrified of something behind the door. Ignoring who it might be, I brought her back into our kitchen, sat her down and then, as always, climbed on her knee. Being so young, all I could do was hold her and I'm sure that's what I did. Held her until whatever it body-trembling was had passed. May had been experiencing panic attacks and dizzy spells for some time, but always outside. Suddenly the world had become too big and dangerous for her; after this incident she never voluntarily left the house again. She developed severe agoraphobia, so much so, even a knocking on the front door could on occasion completely freak her out.

I've only fleeting memories of her/us before this happened, of before she became psychologically housebound. Howling laughing, May and Annie King dancing in from the bingo, putting sherbet sweet Swizzles with inked numbers on them into an old rectangular biscuit tin. Me then enthusiastically raiding that rectangular biscuit tin to eat the ink-numbered Swizzles (ink-numbered Swizzles were what she used to mark her bingo card – long before the trusty felt-tipped dabber it was ha'penny sweets). I've shaded whispers of May janglin' in Mrs Dreah's; I loved those nights. Also, us both visiting her friend along 'n' around the same landing, and me passionately obsessed with her friend's big, black, patent leather handbag. I loved the noise of the elegantly shaped, shining metal clicking mechanism holding the bag together and was repeatedly opening 'n' snapping it shut, then feverously rooting through and, to the embarrassed sound of May's repeated apologies, pulling out its contents... 'Oh, I'm sorry about this Mary, he's a bloody nuisance around handbags, never outta mine. I'll drag 'im home in a minni!' I can still smell the thick powder-puff scent of that particular handbag. It nostalgically clings to me like perfumed fog. I've a few flashes of holding her hand whilst out shopping in Greaty (Scouse for 'Great Homer Street Market'), but that's it; memories of my mother are mostly all inside. She must have thought it safer somehow. That being inside kept bad things outside. If only.

The Grand National, like Friday's pocket money payday, was as important a cultural event as Christmas. Actually, no – if payday was Christmas, then The Grand National felt like an extra New Year's Eve. It was a collectively massive do, one of those we could all join in on, and my favourite memory of a Blackstock Gardens' May Butler. The square itself was fire-cracking with the furore of it all, the landings alive with people toing and froing from flat to flat. With so much going on, it also felt a bit like St. Patrick's Day, but instead of driving out snakes we were gambling on horses. *The Pink Echo* (our local news-paper's racing/sports paper) was dutifully bought; my brothers and their mates were in our flat boozing, everybody's upbeat vocally buoyant, then the talk of what horses to put on with our Jimmy and John being the more knowing of racetrack form. I trusted our Jimmy 'n' John implicitly, but was gonna to pick my horse the way me Ma picked hers: the tried and trusted safety-pin method. This meant, with eyes tight shut, taking an opened safety-pin, circling it high above the list of horses and then blindly stabbing it into *The Pink Echo*. Wherever the safety-pin landed was the horse you'd bet on. I remember Big John saying, 'Now Gerrid, d'ye want me to put this on each way for ye?' Not knowing what he meant, I stubbornly said *no* and that I deffo wanted my horse to win. 'Alright Gerrid, y'wanna win, I know tha', we all wanna win lad, but if it comes second, third or fourth, on each way you'll get a birra money back.' Being my mother's son, I stood my ground insisting I wanted it to win. 'Okay Gerrid, okay, your choice. It's an outsider and most probably won't, but I'll put it on to win for ye.' With our John being the most diplomatic of my brothers, he did just that. It must have been my first ever bet because I had never been so excited about putting a bet on. To be honest, I'm not too sure I knew what a bet was, but because everybody else was so infectiously thrilled with it all so was I. There were journeys to the betting office, to the ale-'ouse, with us once again playing outside the pub, hoping for a spare tanner or a packet of crisps. A carnival camaraderie coloured everywhere; something about the day dynamically enthusing everyone. That is until the race was called.

In 6A Blackstock Gardens, just before The Grand National set off, you could hear that horse-picking safety-pin drop, but soon as the starting gun fired, all hell broke loose. By this time the flat was full of brothers, their wives, girlfriends, mates and the noise from them, little less than roaring. A difficult noise to successfully describe. Let's call it a colourfully animated improvisational sound, with hands violently punching/thumping the air and lots of effusively meant swearing at failing or falling horses. People were literally leaping from their chairs, seeming to me like one of those fairground games where you'd smash down a mallet on some peg only for another one to immediately pop back up somewhere else. Chaos in abundance, but it was the safest chaos in the world and certainly the most entertaining. Soon as the race had finished, there were a lot of grumpy, upset faces, but in amongst the four-letter-worded griping Big John said, 'Wait a minni, I think our Gerrid's won 'ere.' And I had. The rank outsider I'd picked with me Ma's safety-pin had won The Grand National. There was cheering and being lifted up, a tonne of speeding hands rubbing my hair and calls of *y'one jammy little bastard you! Eh, 'ow fuckin' jammy's our Gerrid!*

Much later on, with my already half-pissed brothers spruced up in their Saturday best and about to set off into town for their weekending shenanigans, May proudly took it upon herself to award me my Grand National winnings. In front of everybody she ceremoniously placed in my hands a whole half a crown. Wrapping my tiny fingers tight around my winnings, she said, 'There y'go lad, look at that, just for you. Now don't go spendin' it all in one shop, d'ye hear me?' I can't begin to tell you how over the moon I was at this half a crown; they were big coins for small hands, coins you could hardly hold, and I'd only gone 'n' won one! Although I didn't spend it all in the one shop, with my nephews John 'n' Stephen I immediately flew over to Linda's on Vauxhall Road. You could buy a lot of comics, sweets and bottles of lemo with half a crown and still have change for more the following day. We'd have sat on *the metty*, a long rectangular hole in a local factory wall with an elongated cold metal sill. There were two next door holes with metal sills, one of them much narrower, where we'd often play buses. Just won The National, a bottle of cream soda, tonnes of sweets and crisps, playing buses with my nephews on the metty, *ding ding...* what more could any winning kid want? Well, he might have wanted a bit more of his winnings actually! Much later on, May confessed to me on that on Grand National Day I'd won a lot more than half a crown: 'It was more like a good few quid lad, but you'd 'ave just spent it on stupid sweets, so I pocketed the rest.' We laughed it off, but she'd always jemmy in her tagline... 'D'ye remember that 'orse's name lad?' I'd always have to say *yes* and with her trademark hissing laugh, May would screech, 'Gay Trip, Gerrid, it was called Gay Trip, an' you've been on one ever since!'

I like to think, after The Grand National and playing on the metty with our Little John 'n' Stephen, that when she called me in for the night something with her was a-magically brewin'. Standing over the grate to whoosh back up a waning coal fire, with both hands, May was holding a double-sided piece of our broadsheet *The Pink Echo*. I loved how the glow of the fire grew behind the newspaper before, like an exploding sun, it flared and dramatically burst into flames. Because May liked to entertain, she then comedically faffed and panicked about, hurriedly hand-fanning what was left of the fast-burning paper into the fire. It looked amazing as bits of newspaper, like Shakespearian faeries, backdraft flew up the flu of our chimney... a gay trip indeed. To me it was a lot like a spell; she was a lot like a witch. Before starting school, with fairytales 'n' prayers she taught me to read, and it was me Ma making that dying coal fire come alive again. I do wonder if, after the celebratory madness of The Grand National, she was putting on a May Butler stage-managed magic show.

Writing about your mother is a strange thing. You can't quite get over the feeling of snitching. I'm not telling tales out of school; I'm telling my story, hers, ours, and it was/is *ours*. What I feel about all this, and believe when I say there are lot more tales to come, is just how much mammoth life-story she'd already had. My four-foot-ten mother was and will forever be legendary to me. She wasn't always a good or gentle legend, far from it, but ungentle or otherwise I wouldn't have been brought up by any other legend or indeed mother. At her exceptional best May Butler was kind, loving, witty, always generous and, above all, wise.

When I was a kid, she gave me the best piece of anarcho-socialist advice in the world: 'Always be kind to tramps Gerrid, because y'never know lad, they might be God in disguise.'

I've lived my life by the magical warmth inherent in her advice.

IV

The Sons of May Butler: Jimmy

'Jimmy was frightened of no fucker, Gerrid!'

That's what Big John would say. Much later on, long after everything and in the Throstles Nest pub on Scottie Road, that was our John's abiding memory of his and my oldest brother. As a kid, I *knew* our Jimmy wasn't frightened of any fucker, but he was never *that* Jimmy to me.

Our Jimmy 'n' Big John would have first-hand witnessed the deaths of their brother/sister Vincent/Joan, me Da leaving me Ma, and the social/emotional/financial poverties further punctuating those tormenting experiences. As oldest children, they'd have seen the physically/mentally-deteriorating effect those complicating scenarios would have on their mother. Looking back now, I clearly see that in our Jimmy. Yes, he wasn't frightened of any fucker, but it wasn't all about street fighting. Every fucker round our way street fought. It was also about protecting himself and his family.

There was no such thing as mental health counselling back then and if there was it definitely wasn't for the working class. You were just hit by the shit life hurled and if you could you'd plough through. Safe to say our Jimmy ploughed through with his fists. 'Gerrid, no matter how big they were or how many, Jimmy would take them all on. He had no fear lad, no fear. I've seen him chase away gangs.' Our John's hero stories of his beloved older brother were just that, heroic. Where I come from that's something to be proud 'n' shout about. Where I come from, it was something you more than sometimes had to be. Add to it the bravado/swagger of being a first-time-around, nineteen-fifties, teenageing teddy-boy, the no frills/no shit humour, the drainpiped 'tude 'n' Brylcreem-quiff'd demeanour. Then somewhere in all of that youthful street-scrapping bluster 'n' new urban pop culture, you'd find our Jimmy.

Until I arrived on the scene, all my brothers were keen, good footballers. But our Jimmy was exceptional. Me Ma would say people came from all over to watch him play, telling me they literally wanted to steal him from whomever he was football-ing with to play for their teams. In a bloated, maternal, wood-pigeoning way, May would full-face coo just how proud she was, 'Seriously lad, he'd have all these men there just for him. On the sidelines pointin', showin' their mates how skilled he was, clappin' his every move on the pitch.'

Jimmy was told numerous times he could easily turn pro and at one point high-ups from Everton or Liverpool Football Clubs (maybe even both at the same time) were more than interested. I don't know why, but our Jimmy didn't want to be a professional footballer. And what our Jimmy wanted to do, he defiantly did.

Although towering over me, Jimmy was the smallest of my brothers, but acted the tallest. If you take the scientific physicality of height out of the equation, he clearly was. His was the natural authority of being the first-born successor to his father's vacant but still warm throne. When Big Jimmy Butler left me Ma, it was big brother Little Jimmy taking up the flack. I was far too young to know myself, but I'm reliably informed our Jimmy was the muscle and our John the comedian. May would tell me there was an intensity to Jimmy the rest of us didn't quite have. She'd say it in a slightly concerned, middle-distanced way, like she knew a little something more, but couldn't or wouldn't quite actualise it... 'Sometimes Gerrid, it was like he was carrying the weight of the world on his shoulders.' My guess is sometimes he was.

I loved our Jimmy for the childishly selfish reason that he loved me. When he popped into 6A Blackstock Gardens I immediately felt an overjoyed safer. Not that I was in any imminent danger or unsafe in the knowledge my other brothers wouldn't step in front of a bullet for me; they without hesitation would. It's that out of them all, our Jimmy felt a more definite father figure. At our family get togethers, real dad Big Jimmy Butler would be passionately talked about by his sons, with me being the only son in the room not knowing who he was. Him simply being *me Da* was never enough information. From a very early age that hurt me and, more especially, May. Because so physically knitted to my mother, whenever her estranged husband was mentioned I could feel her body gently convulse, silently sob, her right arm secretly tightening behind my back and pulling me into her side. At five to seven years old, you don't intellectually know what this response to hurt is, but you most certainly know it's emotionally present. An unfamiliar, unwelcome, gnawing presence, weighing you down. A claw of scarring scratches making us both feel ugly and alone.

Always perfectly turned out, our Jimmy looked incredibly glamorous; my memory of his clothes, dark, sleek 'n' neat. He completely rocked those just-ironed white shirts and trademark, fitted, cotton cardigans. His shiny hair, half-quiffing at the top of his good-looking head, a naturally curling black bunch of well-quaff'd grapes. I loved all things American and our Jimmy looked kind of American; Scouse American, Irish/Italian New York American, like he should have his own cop show. He walked like he was the oldest brother, sat like he was the oldest brother, even rubbed 'n' warmed his arse on our coal fire like he was the oldest brother. I'm glimpsing his silhouette as I type, his shadow on the wall, and can still see/sense how defiantly slim, aquiline, always ready to leap up and attack it was. There weren't any creases.

Historically, my family were not great with the authorities, be that school, police or army. So, setting a long-standing familial tradition with school, police and army, our Jimmy was the first of us not to be great or gracious with them. In fact, and to be brutally honest, he was behaviourally bad with authority. You've got to remember, ours was a financially impoverished familial clan with very few material possessions, living in an area housing the Dock Road. The Dock Road being the main traffic artery and home of Liverpool's then thriving docklands and port; a docklands/port containing plenty of worldwide gathered material goods. Put those two equally contrasting realities together and you've a historically-linked, culturally-vivid, symbiotic partnering that, with a li'l bit of scallywagging intellectualism, neighbourly bonds the needs of both parties' skillsets perfectly. In a nutshell, the docks were easy to rob.

May would tell me the police would often come knocking on her door asking for our Jimmy and, because she knew the officers by name, she always had to have a million differing excuses as to why he wasn't there. As they always do, and especially when knowing arresting officers by name, the excuses ran out and our Jimmy ended up in an *approved school*. Although it wasn't, we all called it Borstal, both of those establishment monikers being used to describe a big chunk of his publicly-funded, not-so-private education. Although the first, he wouldn't be the last of my ragtag siblings to reside in high-calibre halls of such distinct physical learning. So school was without doubt a no-no, the police were often punched or ran away from, and the poor army didn't fare too well either. It's an ongoing fact of life; some people in this world just don't respond gently to being told what to do. It's safe to say, after he joined, our Jimmy didn't last long in the army.

*

Janet Gregory was completely gorgeous, her glowing blonde bouffant'd beehive expertly of the time, and when sunlight-backlit, saintly as a Scottie Road halo. If Doris Day was a fit, streetwise Scouser, she'd be our Janet. There is a fantastic photo of Jimmy 'n' Janet slicing their wedding cake, and swear down, if only in my head, it's truly an iconic image. Fuck off the Beckhams; you've nothing on Jimmy 'n' Janet Butler! They just look so great together, completely complimenting one another, 'n' one of my favourite ever photies in the world.

The Gregorys lived on the opposite side of our second red brick bouquet, the *other square*. The other square was probably bigger than the square where we normally played, but because it didn't have long, communal landings for family to look over (it was all windows), we played in it a lot less. Like in the old days when a house might have a living room to everyday exist in and a parlour for Sunday best, the other square acted like our outdoor Sunday best. Funny, thinking back, we did play in it more on a Sunday. Janet was from a large family of brothers/sisters and like many big families of the time dominated by a powerfully placed matriarch. I knew Mrs Gregory and recall her sat Queen-Mother-throne-like with everybody busying their carefully best busy around her. In those days, elderly parents were always looked after by their grown-up kids; it was just what was done, what was expected. Lots of families had a grandmother, grandfather, and sometimes even an auntie/uncle living with them.

Because of May's agoraphobia, our Jimmy 'n' Janet would play a huge part in shaping and moving along my early childhood. They were often around at 6A because there was always something having to be done. My mother didn't take me to school for the first time, so it would have been Janet or Mary Mac. Same with my first confession, first Holy Communion, or things like school/holiday clothes, or going to visit Father Christmas at Sturla's/Blackler's/Lewis's grottos. All those then signature maternal things were done by my sisters-in-law. That was probably the single greatest thing about those tenements; your immediate family were nearby-dotted about and, of course, all of their relations. For example, our John 'n' Stephen's cousins, the Floods, the Murphys, the Edwards and our Janet's nephews the Carneys would all play together, making it feel like a huge extended family. One of the best gifts to me from our Janet was her younger sister Kathleen Gregory. Although not blood- or marriage-related, I always thought of her as kin.

Looking back, I'm realising just how impetuously inquisitive a kid I must have been. I was always up to something, with May never being able to turn her back on me for too long. I remember one particular incident mostly because of how much it was familiarly retold, but what I still physically recall is the immediate searing pain.

Those old tenements all had black metal ranges as fireplaces, with a roaring coal fire heating up certain compartments. There was an oven/stove and what we'd now call a hotplate. Always on that hotplate a big, rusty, old metal iron and a perennially just-brewed pot of tea. The iron and teapot sat precariously together; beleaguered, embattled neighbours, not unlike Elsie Tanner and Ena Sharples. I clearly remember our tea pot, a battered pewter affair with a thick, reddened Bakelite handle (obviously Elsie). I'm a complete tea-aholic and always have been, my tannin addiction starting from extremely early in childhood. May would often say that as a baby I preferred tea to milk, holding onto my rubber-teated, tea-filled beer bottle for dear life. Back in the sixties, babies' milk feeders were often old beer bottles with a shop-bought rubber teat jammed over the top. Pretty certain mine must've been an old Guinness bottle. Like tea, I've been greedily gulping it ever since.

So, I'm very young, the family's in, and our trusty teapot, like a tatty tea siren, is hypnotically calling me to the range. As I'm a cha-loving toddler thinking the quickest route to simply getting a brew must be by grabbing the teapot, I do. I don't fully remember doing that, but most certainly do remember the scorching scalding of my shoulder and immediately screeching the house down. I was then instantly scooped up by our Jimmy, with both Jimmy 'n' Janet taking me to our nearest hospital, The Northern. Afterwards, our Jimmy was furious with my mother, abruptly telling her, 'It could have been his fuckin' face.' Typically vain Butler logic to be more concerned about the face than anything else! Later on, and I think to alleviate long-buried guilt, May would often suggest I'd experienced something of a minor miracle: 'Yeah, y'shoulder got the full whack Gerrid, but there wasn't a single blister on y'hands. Someone was definitely looking down on you lad.' I still bear a sizeable scald scar on my left shoulder.

The exact same thing happened when trapping my finger in our Chris's bike chain. Of course, followed by my operatic screeching and our Jimmy 'n' Janet once again having to rush me to The Northern. You can clearly see why I saw them as parental. They were just that and I dearly loved them for it. Pretty sure our Chris got a well-deserved, well-aimed *Jimmy dig* in the ribs for leaving his upturned bike in our kitchen. Our Chris would fondly tell me about his well-deserved, well-aimed Jimmy digs. I'm probably the only brother to never have received a well-deserved, well-aimed Jimmy dig.

It wasn't all cups of Rosy Lee and cosy accidents, there were relationship hiccups too. Blackstock Gardens was soon to be demolished and by 1970 people had already begun to move out. Jimmy and Janet had got themselves a place in the faraway, sprawling new town of Kirkby. I don't think they liked it much because they were always visiting their respective families back in Blackie. One evening they were both at me Ma's and our Jimmy must have thought it would be a great idea to take me to stay with them in Kirkby for the night. I was a stubborn child and would only do what I wished, so must have enthusiastically wanted to go. My gut instinct was telling me May wouldn't have liked that one bit. Me 'n' me Ma were mentally and bodily conjoined at the spiritual/physical hip. Unless outside with friends, I was seldom out of her sight. More than that, she was now completely agoraphobic and, even at this early age, all kinds of *other* dependant on me. She would not have liked me being away from her one bit and would have certainly communicated that, but our Jimmy would have been as equally immovably insistent.

I loved the long journey to Kirkby, adored buses, and being on one in the dark with my big brother 'n' sister-in-law was the most thrilling thing. There is something about speeding past flickering/strobing street/shop lights in a bus completely captivating to the magpie imaginings of kids; it felt like a funfair ride or, even better, travelling through time. When we arrived at Jimmy/Janet's everything must have been fine; they would have treated me like kid-brother gold. What I clearly remember though is when it was time to go to bed. I completely and hysterically lost all control and totally broke down. From being a happy-go-lucky little brother, I became a screeching, bawling, sobbing heap.

I now recognise it as separation anxiety, but you must remember that back then there was no such thing as mental health, just life and how you pushed through it. I was uncontrollably weeping and wanting to get back to my mother. It must have been a nightmare for them both because I just couldn't settle, keeping them awake well into the wee small hours. I was all but broken with whatever it was and how I felt about whatever it was, so it would have looked like abject fear, perhaps of them, rejection even. It must have been horrible, especially for our Jimmy; it would have deeply saddened him. I can still feel that panicking whelping now, its terrifying, debilitating intensities. I've not cried like it since.

The next morning came and I was hiding behind my mousy-brown fringe and deeply, sheepishly ashamed. A wanting to immediately disappear and instantly not be there kind of ashamed. A hoping the ground would do us all the biggest favour and swallow me whole kind of ashamed. A gruelling series of despairing emotions and I painfully knew I'd done something terribly wrong. They were both working the next day and our Janet wasn't in any way pleased with me, so very soon after getting up they took me straight home. The bus journey back wasn't quite so thrilling. There were no flickering/strobing fairground rides, no mercurial time travel; in fact, that uncomfortably *present* moment was defined by an angry and disappointed silence. For about a week I was in the doghouse with our Janet and that upset me; I think it was the first time I'd ever felt the full whack of embarrassment. Our Jimmy was fine, he always was, although it took a little time to get our Janet's trust back. But when I did everything was exactly the same.

Afterwards, when Jimmy told our Ma what had happened and how I'd behaved, I remember a snake-eyed May being an almost-gloating smug. Climbing behind her on our favourite chair, I heard her, half-smirking, say, 'Told y'not to take him away from me, didn't I lad.' She could occasionally be a bit of a cackling auld sorceress could May.

My memories of our Jimmy are mostly being joyfully lifted by him; he always held me up. No sooner was I in his arms than he'd kind of arm roll me up his chest and then I'd magically be on his shoulders. There is an oldest brother/youngest brother, laughing/giggling intimacy to that bodies-travelling physicality that's just both yours. The shaking of the hair, being held under his arm like a sack of coal, swung out by the arms… a never-ending sense of familial bonding and feeling safe. I relished the safety of being by/with our Jimmy, especially when walking into town and his big hand at the back of my little head, tucking me into his striding legs with me skip-like hurrying to keep up. For all his fists, for all his fighting bravado, he cared deeply. He knew I didn't have a dad, how it confused me, and I was very much aware of that. It was something we silently understood about each other. One of many wonderful things about much older big brothers was you seldom needed words.

Our Jimmy loved kids and desperately wanted his own. It wasn't happening and was a cause of some concern between him and Janet. I remember our Jimmy saying to me Ma, 'Our fuckin' John's two kids with another on the way, an' I 'aven't even got one yet.' (Their sibling rivalry wasn't always football and whose were the best winklepickers or quiff.) Then May replying, 'Don't worry lad, it'll 'appen one day, worryin' won't 'urry it along. A watched kettle never boils.' And happen one day it brilliantly did. Janet fell pregnant and both she and our Jimmy were overjoyed. I'm pretty sure there was a party, but then there were always parties. Although a *definite occasion* was always a great excuse for a boozy celebration, we never let anything scatter-cushion commonplace as *occasion* get in the way of throwing one. When our Cathy was born, we probably had another do, several of them. Jimmy and Janet had a daughter and never a happier couple could there be. Janet had sisters, but Cathy was the first girl on our side of the family; my mother being XYY chromosome-plagued by a succession of troublesome boys. There was something about her being the first girl really hitting home, especially to May. Jimmy adored his daughter; always bringing her over to proudly show off to his mother. I'm pretty sure it was in 6A Blackstock Gardens our Cathy took her first steps. So sure, I wrote a poem about it. I love that poem. But ain't life a mightily complicated thing? A tricky, untrustworthy blighter, so it is. No sooner does it offer you the world, it can just as easily take it from you.

Last time I saw our Jimmy was one weekday morning. He'd often pop in to see May before setting off to work on the demolition. Whatever our Jimmy was feeling you immediately saw/felt it too. He wore his emotions in his body and on his face. He was visibly perturbed and sad that morning, taking May off into the hallway to have a private word. They had an almost psychic oldest son/first child bond and telling-each-other-important-things relationship. It was only for a short time and through a not-quite-closed door I could hear their intense, concerned mumblings. Then, like everything was fine, he brotherly bounded in, shook my hair and said, 'I'll see y'later Jelly Beans.' May didn't tell me what was said, but worriedly, under her breath told me, 'He's not right, Gerrid, Jimmy's not right.'

Our Jimmy's favourite song was a mournful lament of a ballad called 'Nobody's Child'. An odd song choice for a rough 'n' ready ex-teddy-boy, mightily big on the rockin' 'n' rollin' brav-ado of his knockabout youth culture. The chorus lyrics go...

> "I'm nobody's child, I'm nobody's child
> Just like a flower I'm growing wild
> No mommy's kisses and no daddy's smile
> Nobody wants me, I'm nobody's child."

I completely get why he loved it. I wish he'd become a profess-ional footballer.

V
The Sons of May Butler: Big John

Nothing to do with a slightly rewritten version of Robin Hood, Big John was called that because he named his first born after himself. So, *his* first child instantly became *Little* John, and *he*, as father, immediately became *Big* John. Whoever was named after a parent, especially a first born, automatically became the *little* version of them both and that would never change. Even when the littler version would soon tower over the big one… it's an anglicised Irish-Scouse thing.

Big John Butler was handsome. I'm talking pure/proper matinee idol handsome. Our Jimmy was too, but he was more a rough 'n' ready Jimmy Cagney-esque rogue. Big John Butler was a dreamy smooth, nineteen-fifties-looking crooner. That's where the likeness to Bobby Darin ends because, more than anything, our John was a whirlwinding comedic vaudevillian. Big John would always say he couldn't stand to see anyone unhappy and so, with raucous cyclonic energy, be it a christening, wedding or funeral (go-to working class occasions), he'd do just that; make everybody happy. Not in a naff, annoying way, but properly, like a skilled comedian or expert clown. His naturally innate abilities to lift the mood or make somebody sing 'n' dance were legendary in our family's history. He'd outwardly rejoice at the prospect of a family do, at getting a party started; often before the party had begun. More than me even, John Winston Butler should've been in the show business; his untrained yet perfectly pitched vaudevillian skillsets extraordinary as entertaining. I'd sit/stand in completely entertained awe at how he expertly worked a room. Like Judy Garland or Sammy Davis Jr might excitably be waiting in the wings for the big-band overture to bring them on stage, Big John behaved in a not too dissimilar fashion. He'd be impatiently waiting outside a door, then energetically quick-step enter the pub or party like he was raring to sing 'Swanee'. And he often did sing 'Swanee'. My earliest memory is of him at some family do, vigorously rubbing the tops of his legs like he was revving them up to magnificently Gene Kelly tap-dance, and saying, 'Well Gerrid, 'ere we go kid, show time.'

Big John Butler was Methuselah the teddy-boy, never fully growing away from what he held so youth and counter-culturally dear. Although our Jimmy still sported a semi-quiff, he'd definitely stopped being a teenager. Our still perfectly full-quiff'd Big John defiantly hadn't. He was encyclopaedic in his knowledge of his youth culture and a gloating, boasting, confident in what it meant to him. Big John Butler was the teenager he needed to be at exactly the right time he could be it. He loved all the bootleg American music coming over from the States and, because it so often wouldn't reach our record shops, he'd sometimes have to get it off the ship it had sailed in on. In those days, American 7" singles were like illegal drugs, carrying that same money-exchanging, narcotic, night-time slyness to get them. There was something of the auld romantic poet about our John: he was able to verbally make dark, wet, fifties dockland dusks sound like the best, most atmospherically evocative nights in the world. So much so, I wanted to be there too. So vividly all-encompassing his storytelling, I think I was. He was of that Scouse seafaring, tall-tale-weaving, generously jangling vibe. The exact same vibe singing a note-perfect 'My Way' and making a two-minute pub joke last long as The Old Testament.

In many ways Jimmy 'n' John were chalk 'n' cheese. The

characterfully vivid intensities plaguing our Jimmy seemed nowhere near John. I'm not saying he didn't have any hidden intensities, he must have, but what Big John Butler did have in his more jocular possession was a very necessary forcefield. He never flew off the handle and wasn't in any way violent; whenever there were rows (and there were plenty) he was always the main peacemaker. Whilst Jimmy was able to handle chaos with his fisting temper, our John, always hands-free, seemed able and with graceful passivity to leisurely glide through it. They'd argue like oldest siblings do, but lovingly recognised each other's qualities and shortfalls. Again, the ease and naturalness of familial symbiosis; Big John was able to calm Jimmy down and Jimmy always had his back. How we say in the 'pool, *job done!*

Although they must have, I don't remember Jimmy or John living in 6A; they'd moved out and married long before I discovered memory (or did memory discover me?). I'd just been born when Big John got hitched to his teen-hood sweetheart Mary McMahon. Oh wow, our Mary, warra broad! Like Janet Gregory, Mary Mac was so completely of the sixties. A strong, handsome-looking woman who when riled could stick out her hand and stop a fleet of oncoming Sherman tanks. Even very young, and I'm talking early twenties, our Mary was a more than formidable force of street-born supernature. That's not to say she wasn't other things like kind and funny; she was extremely kind, hysterically funny, one of the funniest. But blimey, you didn't mess with her.

On the telly there here was an all-girl singing group called The Ladybirds and I always thought our Mary looked just like the one with glasses. Like the one in the glasses, Mary also sported an amazing beehive, wore great figure-hugging clobber, and was able to work those horn-rimmed specs like a swingin' sixties winner. There's another personally iconic photie of Janet and Mary Butler standing atop the steps in a red brick entrance of one of Blackstock Gardens' stairwells, perfectly capturing their youthful relationship. Stood side-by-side, beehive-by-beehive, blonde, brunette, completely of the time but expertly themselves, both holding ciggies and smiling. Nothing posed, completely natural, two young sixties women content in each other's laughing company. In the eternally chaotic bedsitting room of my imagination, it hangs like a poster covering a damp spot on a wall.

Some years later I'd meet and befriend actively feminist women who would talk of working-class women as oppressed by men. Now, I'm not arguing with or in any way disputing that. I wholly believe in the historically corrosive infrastructures of an out-of-all-control, controlling, capitalistic patriarchy, but I did wonder if they'd ever met any Scottie/Vauxhall Road women. Fiscally/physically, abusive-patriarchy impacted (how could it not?), but some women, like Mary Mac, would readily stand up too and, if pushed, knock any abusive-patriarchal knob-'ead into the middle of next week. There is a physically-charged, fist-fighting-back fearlessness to a lot of those women which has gone unrecognised in our written histories. I can honestly say I never grew up with the notion women were in some way physically/mentally/intellectually inferior to men, not at all.

Like Jimmy, Big John had spent some time in the army. Honestly, there are wonderful black 'n' white photies of our John with his mates in Kenyan barracks, literally with full quiffs. I'm pretty sure it was mandatory for every would-be National Service soldier to be head-shaven but, soon as he could, Big John Butler grew back his identity-defining, superbly-sculpted, teddy-boy hair. No matter our sibling personalities, and they all differed, there is an instinctive sense of cocksure rebelliousness running through all us Butlers. In a similar way to Jimmy, and I think for similar reasons, Big John Butler didn't serve his full time nor was he ever honourably discharged from the armed forces. In fact, it was the opposite of honourably. The main reason being that when on leave he'd never go back, preferring to spend precious quality time with his beloved and by now betrothed, Mary McMahon; our ballsy, take-no-prisoners Mary Mac being far more important to him than any career the army could provide. That, or maybe he didn't want to ever again relinquish his precious quiff... I wouldn't put it past him.

John 'n' Mary lived two landings above us, birthing my nephews Little John and Stephen. We were never out of each other's flats and, with me being only a year older than Little John, they felt more like younger brothers than nephews. Although I young-uncle adored, I'll never forget my seething jealousy of them both when May, a heavy smoker like everybody back then, had collected enough Embassy ciggie coupons to exchange for gifts from her precious catalogue. Cigarette coupons were a marketed advertising grab used to make people get lung cancer earlier. In another old biscuit tin, bound together with grubby elastic bands, May kept stack after stack of those coupons. I thought they looked like tight, paper bricks, but they were her blue/black/green gold dust; her savings. Every day, if seeing one on the ground, she'd instruct me to pick up an Embassy coupon. Well, the more the merrier, and who knows, probably a little less lung/heart disease.

Pretty sure it was Easter (felt spring-like in the square) and Little John, Stephen and I were all getting gifts off her from the Embassy catalogue. I knew something about these presents, but they were to be complete surprises for my nephews. Even knowing something, I didn't know everything, and was excited as my nephews as to what these much-talked-of prezzies might be. With May being my mother, I must have thought it would be something huge for me and not so huge for them. Well, I couldn't have been wronger. I was furious when they were presented with two funky bicycles with stabilisers and all I got was a flimsy run-of-the-mill scooter. I'd just been taught how to ride a bike (without stupid stabilisers) by their cousin Sharon Flood and bore the scrapes 'n' scratches to prove it, so wasn't best pleased. I clearly remember looking over our landing, almost weeping with jealous rage, as they joyfully rode around the square on their Nan-bought, Embassy-coupon'd bicycles. Don't think I once properly played on that stupid scooter. Remember soon-as-humanly-possible slyly giving it away to some kid from another tenement, then sheepishly coming home to May saying it had been stolen. She'd have given me down the banks (Scouse for 'grief'), probably threatened to reef me, but a telling-off or an ear-ripping reef was fair exchange for being rid of that ridiculously flimsy two-wheeled monstrosity. I grumpily smarted about that useless angular contraption for weeks. The only one clocking my obvious disappointment was a giggling, rubbing-his-hands Big John... 'Never mind eh Gerrid, better luck next time lad.'

May Butler would always bleat she never had a favourite son. I've no doubt she truly believed it, but all her other sons, including me, without doubt knew Big John was exactly that. We each had our own distinctive relationship to May, but no-one lifted her spirits quite like our John. When he entered 6A, she'd become somehow stereotypically more motherly around him. A bit more baking cakes, flour-covered rolling-pin and homemade apple pies; something she certainly wasn't with the rest of us.

No matter our varying ages, we'd all get a good telling off from May, but I never once heard her raise her voice to Big John. Jimmy had been a law-breaking tearaway and our John told me he'd had his light-fingered moments, but perhaps Big John just never got caught. I think that him not bringing trouble to her door and his preternatural comedic ability to make her laugh must have given him a special place in her heart.

Watching them both, I always felt Big John was somehow deliberately softer around May than we were. He was her cushioned corner, so when bumping into him she never hurt herself. A lot of May's darker moods origin'd from hurt. Our

John was big, raucous, and upbeat playful around his brothers/sons but, without altering the temperature of the room, always seemed able to immediately soothe his tensing-up mother. I loved watching it, probably looking for tips; loved all the special 'n' unspoken secrets we individually shared with her. Although blanketly our mother, we all had our own unique shorthand with May and she with us. My sense is, of all her sons, Big John was let into the crumbling fragilities of her thinking more. Out of us all I think she trusted him most.

If one thing above all else defines a Blackstock Gardens' Big John Butler, it's music; he loved music. It wasn't every Friday, but most Fridays he'd after-work pop into 6A with sweets for me, something for May, and brand new records for the record player. Thomas, Chris 'n' Paul would have bought the music of the day – The Beatles, The Rolling Stones – but our John would always bring into the flat his end of pop cultural history. After, say, The Stones' 'Satisfaction', The Beatles' 'Paperback Writer' (my favourite Beatles track), we'd get Lonnie Donegan's skiffle classic, 'Cumberland Gap'. He was a massive Elvis, Chubby Checker, Chuck Berry, Little Richard fan and, always in his hands, a sprawling selection of their glorious back catalogues. More than anybody else though, he'd play and sing/dance along to Buddy Holly. At seven years old, I was as culturally familiar with Peggy Sue and her impending marriage as I was Andy Pandy, Little Ted and Looby Loo's dodgy in-the-basket-threesome. It wasn't only him madcap-boogying to them (he was a bonkers dancer); he'd get me and me Ma grooving along too. Our John was so physically musical, his whole body alive with wild, rhythmically improvised movement. It couldn't just be him bouncing around the house, especially on paydays, it had to be us all bouncing around the house. It was more than simply that though; he was always looking for ways to cheer up May, to keep her entertained. It was no wonder, although she'd never admit it, that Big John was her favourite.

VI

The Sons of May Butler: Thomas

It must have been just after five o'clock and as per I was in our front bouquet skipping with the girls. Without any reservation or embarrassment, I thoroughly adored playing skipping. Not too sure if I'm making this bit up, but I could have been enthusiastically singing the accompanying rhyme louder than any of the other ladies of the rope. I would have been completely lost in the choral excitement of the skipping song, so much so that nothing else would have occupied my mind. You've gotta remember here, I was made from MGM musicals and big band tap numbers, priding myself on being more Ann Miller than Alan Ball. Everything around me was wholly blocked out, except for the wonderfully lyrically/musically-colourful moment I was florally immersed in.

So, imagine my shocked/startled surprise when the ground abruptly moved away from me, not to mention my sudden alarm as the skipping string snapped from my fingers, zig-zagging a whipping, scribbling, wriggle to the floor. Then my indignant rage as I was physically turned away from the game I loved and demonstrably marched towards my dark stairwell home... all this whilst about five feet in the air.

Whatever this monster was it had accomplished something of an expert grab. My arms were splayed immovably outward, my kicking feet unable to connect to either the floor or its shins, the tight choke of my jumper and shirt around my neck seriously inhibited any just-learnt profanities I was desperate to screech. Still in the air, I was frogmarched along our landing, skilfully manoeuvred into the already open door of 6A and, just inside our kitchen, dropped like a stone onto the couch. Thomas Butler then said, 'What's in for tea Ma?'

My brothers, except perhaps for Big John, were all proper hard-knocks, with our Tommy visually being the most surface butchest. In fact, and including me because of the surname Butler, all our nicknames were shortened to either Butch or Buck. So, camp li'l me, without any knowing irony whatsoever, was often called Butch. Our Butch (Thomas) took his obvious masculinity a little more seriously than my other brothers. I always thought if the Butlers were the Wombles, then big Butch Tommy Butler would be the near-named, big-butch Tomsk. But not for the likes of us those mythical, evergreen, litter-strewn park-scapes of Wimbledon Common, no, just the masculine, wide-backed, fist-smashing majesty of Blackstock Gardens. Ooh, go on now ducky, how was tha' for a birra Butch?

Our Tommy loved the bones of me, but if my girlygoo fey ways irked anybody most, it was him. Even when picking me up by the scruff of the neck like a cat might an escaping kitten, there wasn't any malice. He'd have, without effort or bother, plonked me down and simply have said to May, 'I've just caught him playing with the fuckin' girls again.' With me belligerently replying, 'If I wanna play with the girls, I'll play with the girls!' Something about my high-pitched defiance always made our Tommy laugh. Then, gently picking me up, he'd say, 'Gerrid, if you don't change y'ways, y'll soon get into all kinds of trouble. There's rough-'ard arl arse bastards out there waitin' to pick on little kids like you. Probably watchin' y'skippin just then 'n' waitin' to pounce.' In his own masculine way, he was looking after me whilst at the same time trying to toughen me up. You see, he did know and was dead right; the world was gonna be physically difficult for a camp kid like me, and one day he wouldn't be there to hurl me up by the neck of my jumper to protect. All my brothers tried, but it was our Thomas wanting me to properly look after myself the most, and so it was Tommy who gave me fighting 'n' boxing lessons. Pretty sure I'd have told him I much preferred playing hopscotch, gutters or kick-the-can to Queensbury Rules fisticuffs any day but, to give him his dues, every day he'd always give it a go. Fighting and being able to look after yourself, certainly back then and especially in the Vauxhall/Scottie Road end of Liverpool, was fist-clenching, gut-punching currency. And our Tommy knew that in those particular departments I was completely skint. I'm not sure if our Tommy actually boxed, don't think he did, but he may have trained in one of the many surrounding boxing clubs/gyms. I vaguely remember being in them with him, not fighting, but watching; maybe one of his mates owned one. I loved how the nostril-attacking smells of sweat, soap and Old Spice (the aftershave of the day) seemed to permeate everywhere. Although he may have been concerned about my outwardly effete manner, he wasn't in any way ashamed; I would often be alongside him, tucked into his leg, in those more macho places.

Jimmy and Big John had long flown the coup but Thomas, Chris 'n' Paul all lived at 6A Blackstock Gardens with me 'n' me Ma. The odd thing being it was a three-bedroomed flat with May and I in one and all three of them in the other. We did have a spare bedroom bigger than the other two, but kept it just that, spare. Maybe it had damp. Saying that though, there was always tonnes of stuff in there, like bits of broken machinery, half-built bikes and literally tonnes of house-bricks. It also housed a bulging library of Everton football programmes, an old, bright-yellow-painted gramophone carcass and, sometimes, pigeons. Yes, my brothers would on occasion catch and keep mangy old micks (micks being Scouse for 'pigeons' and nadger Scouse for 'sparrow'). It was more their darkened, grubby boys' den than anything else, and I think something proper lads did back then.

Our Thomas looked different to our Jimmy and Big John; he was a real clothes stallion, sartorially much more of-his-time. I clearly remember a lot of the sixties, particularly the latter end, with our Thomas cutting a more-than-stylish dash. His hair, unlike Jimmy's or John's immaculately sculpted quiffs, was not curly/wavy dark, but lanker, more mousy in colour, and worn at a longish side-part. Thomas enjoyed the more expensive boutique clothes; well-designed, fitted leather jackets, thin ties, some subtle jewellery 'n' great shoes; he was quite the dandy. I'll never forget his beautiful gold, black onyx cufflinks; they looked so cool. Sometimes he let me put them on him, telling me, 'You'll be wearing these one day Gerrid.'

Tommy was stockier, heavier-boned than the sinewy, leaner, rest of us; a much more solidly present figure. Being younger than Jimmy 'n' Big John, but the oldest brother in our flat, he bore all the senior authority of that position. He was no wall-flower when it came to speaking out, but characterfully quieter than our Chris or Paul. He was effortlessly and elegantly snazzy though. I remember being outside with him and his mate, all of us stood near his mate's brand new motor. Few people had cars in Blackie, so this little sports number parked by our part of the tenement brought all the kids out to have a look. In Blackie, kids and adults constantly mixed, especially if there was a bit of gratuitous showing-off to do. The best bit of this particular piece of showing-off was when, once all the kids were around the car, our Thomas theatrically put his hand in his pocket and magician-like pulled out a big red/brown ten bob note. Then, right in front of everyone, he gave it to me, saying, 'Ee are Jelly Beans, that's fer you!' Children round our way seldom got ten bob notes, it was always ha'pennies, thru'penny bits, tanners, silver shillings or, at best, a rare half-crown. To be passed one of those enormous pieces of paper by your flash big brother next to his mate's even flashier sports number was a defining kid moment. That ten bob note was huge, the size of a big tawny pillowcase. It might still be the richest I've ever felt.

It could only have been when Thomas left school, probably at fourteen/fifteen, and started work that we got out of the poverty trap I spoke of before. I'm sure Jimmy/John must have given May a little financial dropsy now 'n' again, but they had their own flats/lives/families to feed, clothe and fund. Thomas would have given May some quite substantial weekly keep (Scouse for 'rent'), closely followed by Chris, then Paul. Having three lots of keep coming in every Friday didn't mean you'd always have a silver shilling for the leccy, but meant you could confidently borrow, knowing you could payday pay back. Thinking back, before our Chris left school and started working, and for about a year or maybe even more, our fifteen/sixteen-year-old Tommy would have been my family's main bread-winner.

In his many efforts to butch this particular Butch up, our Tommy would occasionally take me to his footy matches. Sometimes full team, sometimes five-a-side. Thomas and Jimmy both played Saturday/Sunday local league football. Don't get me wrong, it was great to be part of it all, but I was much more interested in what was going on around me than the dreary match. So, if there were girls my age (there were always dads' daughters milling about), I'd be on the grass, cross-legged 'n' circle-sat, hyper-jangling away with them. My brothers could have been scoring skilfully brilliant goal after skilfully brilliant goal and I wouldn't have given a toss; far too busy telling my new girl mates how fabulously expert I was at Two-balls. I did love being in the wide-open, greener outside and travelling on the mesmerising bus journeys getting to and from them, but goal scoring/saving football was never gonna be as engrossing as making a complex series of daisy chains with Carol, my new bezzy from Bootle. I found it far more entertaining in the literally ballsy, gregariously steamy changing rooms, with them all cracking open beers, telling dirty jokes and getting ready for the night-time out. My early childhood was sometimes surrounded by a lot of raucously pissed-up, naked men. Although experientially different, a bit like my later adulthood really.

Our Tommy must've thought that the more football I was introduced too, the more it might seep in, and the more I'd eventually get into it. Again, his efforts were to no avail, but that didn't stop me enjoying tagging along and loving him for trying.

Our Tommy, Chris and Paul were immovable Evertonians, always at familial, football league loggerheads with staunch Liverpudlians, Jimmy and Big John. Seriously, whenever there was a derby match, they'd verbally/physically go hammer 'n' tongs at each other, with me sat in the middle intently pondering the monochrome imagery and narrative legitimacy of Looby Loo's pigtails (how *does* she make them curl up so?).

One fine day, Everton had won some big deal with football, likely a cup or shield, and were going to parade it on an open-top double decker bus down Vauxhall Road. God, what a visually stunning day that one was. Blackstock Gardens was festively awash with blue 'n' white balloons and crêpe paper garlands made by its Everton-supporting fans – only to then be unceremoniously burst 'n' ripped down by the Liverpool-supporting ones.

It was an energised and excitable day, a lot like The Grand National or St. Patrick's, with our Tommy visibly thrilled to be taking me to see his favourite team sporting their newly-won trophy. Vauxhall Road was teeming with a Biblically epic, scarf-waving, partying blue sea of Evertonian Scousers. I was sat upon our Tommy's shoulders and next to us, perched on his wonderfully raucous Auntie Irene's shoulders, my nephew Little John. I had an ice cream, a be-flaked, raspberry-sauce-dripping ninety-niner, and was ridiculously over the moon about being held so high above all this pulsing blue 'n' white majesty. Our Tommy's hands grabbed hold of my knees for security, like I was the winning cup. Once again that big-brotherly feeling of protective safety; I was in a crowd of drunken thousands and it felt great, the safest place on the planet.

As the open-top bus slowly drove up Vauxhall Road, gently gliding past us, the constant singing/cheering/roaring rose further in volume, becoming something extraordinarily else. Thousands of people chorally together in one uplifting voice; a guttural from the earth, from the stomach, from the throat noise, creating a high-flying cheer. A humongously loud, wide-open sound, so full of celebration it was almost too thrilling to be a part of. I hated football with every fibre of my tiny, camp being, but in that moment I genuinely could have exploded with joy.

Apart from wanting me to enjoy the celebrations, there was a sneaky, cunning method in our Tommy's madness. When we got back to 6A he sat me down and said to me, 'Right, now Gerrid, who's y'favourite team an' who d'ya support?' I had never supported any team, don't think I really knew what supporting a team even was, but because I was so grabbed in the excitable-fist-of-moment, I hands-in-air screamed, 'EVERTON!', followed by our Tommy yelling out, 'YEEEEEEES! Now Gerrid, you go tell that to Jimmy an' Big John. Tell them you support the best team in the world!' My brothers were so feverishly competitive around football; I'm now sure our Tommy, in a Machiavellian move, used that event as a winning ruse to trick me into supporting his team. It's not that he didn't mean to give his little brother one of the happiest times of his life but getting another Evertonian onside, was for him, a family victory.

Within whatever memory is or might be, however it shapes, some moments are just complete; this is one of those memories. That day meant everything to me and, from then on, I was the crappiest/campiest Evertonian there ever was... still am.

*

Angela Hollywood was something of a much-needed godsend. Angela was our Tommy's girlfriend and someone new to the Butler family; the first of my brothers' girlfriends (not wives) whom I remember. Like our Tommy, Angela was more *of the time*: big hair but not a beehive; a woman fashionably looking like she was heading toward the newly bourgeoning nineteen-seventies. I recall thinking she was beautiful and like someone off the telly (who that someone off the telly was has gone now, but she would have been gorgeous; it could well have been Judy Geeson).

Angela came from far far away and was brought up in a house with two gardens, so I think our tenement life and oddly shaped family were new to her. She and Tommy would take me to her faraway house and although it wasn't the English countryside of Derbyshire (it was probably Norris Green) it felt like a different world. To me then, faraway countryside meant a bus ride to somewhere slightly less industrially built-up and, perhaps along the way, if lucky, there might be trees by the road. Angela wasn't at all posh, but to this townie, tenement kid, someone with two gardens felt like they resided in Buckingham Palace. I loved visiting the Hollywoods; it seemed like a day out to delightful somewhere I'd never been before, a mini holiday.

I remember Angela's mum and her sister, Imelda. I had never heard a name like that before and immediately loved it. *Imelda*. It had a kind of Arabian Knights, exotic-sounding *otherness*. Imelda, Queen of the Sands, or in my case, Blundellsands. There was a younger brother too, Ian, and we quickly became firm friends.

After a visit to Angela's rather opulent-looking house, our little tenement flat looked and certainly felt a bit more thread-bare than usual. There was a lot of rich colour in her family home, furry wallpaper, bold ornamentation, and thick carpets.

Our beer-/gravy-/tobacco-stained, peeling wallpaper and crumbling-edged, oil-cloth'd floor suddenly appeared not-so-cared-for. Not in a disappointing way, as I loved 6A Blackstock Gardens with all my heart, but suddenly and for the first time, I was made aware there were other places that had much nicer things.

Angela was a concerned-kind to me, taking me under her wing, arms-around-on-knees-chatting, forever smiling, and always with sweets 'n' gifts. I didn't have that many toys or recreational activities; we were a hard knock, rough boys' house without those over-familial, giving/receiving gifting romances, but Angela's brother Ian and their family did. One night, Angela brought a big bag of Ian's old toys for me. There were colouring books, felt tip pens, jigsaws, a games compendium and, what I adored most of all, two bright blue/yellow, battery-operated toy dodgem cars. I thought they were best things/toys I had ever had, that anybody could ever have, and a tonne better than that meffy (Scouse for 'stupid/smelly') scooter me Ma got me off the Embassy catalogue. Even as a young kid, I realised Angela knew I didn't have too much in the way of presents and gifts. I'll never forget her taking me to Lewis's grotto, with me getting my photo taken with Father Christmas. Up until that point, and I was seven mind, it was the first photo ever snapped of me. Angela Hollywood was a wonderful influence for, around, and on me; someone with new ideas and energy. Thomas and Angela would soon become engaged and the idea she'd become another sister-in-law, that she'd be around forever, that she'd indeed be Angela Butler, filled me full of joy.

With all my brothers being proper townies, my young head would be full of tales of their drinking/dancing, pubbing/clubbing adventuring. They made Friday/Saturday nights seem like the best, most electric nights in the world. Even that young, my whole sense of being adult was about one day/night being able to do exactly what they did. That outrageous, boisterously magical thing they had going on with new clothes, showing off, cufflinks, Old Spice, and cool-looking best mates would all, one day, be mine. What made our Thomas stand out from the normal pubbing/clubbing crowd was that he and his best mate were bouncers. Not just everyday bouncers mind, but bouncers on the doors of The Cavern and The Iron Door.

The late-sixties Cavern obviously wasn't the music Mecca it had more recently and spectacularly been, but remained a lot of Scousers' favourite nightclub. But it was The Iron Door, number one ace hotspot of the time, where all their townie action was. Of course, I didn't actually know anything about nightclubs, but knew they were all-important to my brothers and an almost secretive something about nightclubbing was the best thing ever created. The greatest thing for me, because of him being this awe-inducing thing called *a bouncer*, was thinking that our Tommy and his bezzy mate ruled clubs; they were the ones actually controlling them. It was just my wild imaginings, but something now tells me I wasn't that far off.

Our Chris once told me that Thomas had got Jimmy a job on The Iron Door's door, but he had to be quickly taken off because, when it came to bouncing, Jimmy Butler was, shall we say, more than a little enthusiastic. It was complete kudos in the square, especially with mates; your brother was this fantastic thing called a bouncer in nightclubs where their brothers/ sisters partied every weekend; it was like you knew something they didn't. As you've probably gathered by now, it didn't take much to make me feel self-important. Being a Scouser, self-important's hot-wired into in our collective DNA. I was forever telling tall tales to mates about me actually being in those clubs and, because our Tommy, my big butch brother was on the door, how I was the only kid allowed in.

On the surface, our Thomas's and my mother's relationship was like all the brothers, but these two instances mark out something a touch different, perhaps something a little bit more than just surface.

As previously intimated, when riled May Butler didn't hold back. As a brotherhood we knew this and quietly understood never to upset her (or, at the very least, not to try). There was a collective sibling knowledge that she'd already been through too much life-shit and not one of us wanted to suffer that accusatory shrieking, hacking voice of hers ever again. Like most Catholic, Scouse, older women of the time, May was one part Virgin Mary and nine parts clawing, revenging banshee. Whilst arguments would always occur, they were often small and petty – *Ma, wha's in for tea, been waitin' fuckin' ages 'ere* kind of things, with May snappily replying, 'Cows cocks 'n' onions, all y's deserve!' This time though, it was different. The angriest I'd ever seen my mother and the angriest I'd ever witnessed a brother with her.

I have no idea how it came about; all I remember is the titanic clashing and near violent confrontation. I was on the couch (I think with Little John) and, as suddenly as suddenly could sudden, May and Thomas were screaming blue murder at each other. Because of its instant yelling volatility, whatever this was about must have been a long-brewing big. They were almost nose to nose and getting even closer, feeling more like a street fist-fight between two big boxing bruisers than a family row, with May even rolling up the sleeves of her cardigan to properly weigh in. I wish I could recall what our Thomas was saying; my guess is he was telling her to back off and sit the fuck down. When enraged, May could get into fiery, repetitive bludgeoning mode, belting out the same thing over and over again; something personally defamatory to emotionally disable you. She was doing exactly that, repeatedly screaming the one phrase that would seriously affect the macho sensibilities of our Tommy: 'Go on then lad, hit me go on, hit me, hit a woman would ye, that's what you wanna to do isn't it, it's all you fuckin' can do! Go on then, do it, hit me, or are you too much of a fuckin' shithouse, yeah, y'heard me, shithouse!' Our Tommy was anything but a shithouse (shithouse being Scouse for 'coward') and I could see his usually calm face blood-redden, a ready-to-explode crimson, looking like he could genuinely knock her out. At this point May was manically screaming *shithouse, shithouse, shithouse* into his face. Reaching down to our fireplace, Tommy took the thick, metal poker from its grate and, with his hands either ends, right in front of her face, slowly bent it into a U shape. Undeterred and completely unimpressed by our Tommy's show of brute force, May carried on: *shithouse, shithouse, shithouse*. Looking like he was about to hit her with it, Thomas lifted the now bent poker above his head and hurled it forward. The poker flew past, hairsbreadth-missing May's still shithouse squawking head, and smashed through our kitchen window. Because everything was steam-rollering out of all control (and, I think, to stop himself from flattening her), my raging big brother then stormed out of 6A, the slam of our front door so powerfully meant that the whole of Blackstock Gardens shook. Left stranded in an atmosphere dense with a tension new even to me, we sat in tightened/frightened silence. After a few eternity-lasting seconds, May fumed, 'Right, I'm puttin' the kettle on, who wants a cuppa tea? But if that thing knocks, it's not gettin' back in. That's one fuckin' little shithouse tha'!' No one dared utter anything in reply or even audibly slurp the tea almost thrown onto our laps, but something massive had just happened and none of us knew what. The silence was properly broken when May ordered me to fly downstairs and retrieve the now horseshoe-shaped poker. 'Pokers don't buy themselves Gerrid, so he'd better be able to bend it back again or there'll me more fuckin' murder, I'm tellin' ye!'

Next day couldn't have been any more different. It was a beautiful, summer-sun shining afternoon, feeling exactly like a Sunday should. One of those balmy summer days able to soft-blur and rose-tint anything and everything around. Even surrounding factories romantically hazed like they were being filmed by a Vaseline-covered lens. There was just me, May and our Tommy sat in 6A and whatever the night before was about had now almost completely passed. I could tell by their tentatively softer demeanours they were, in their own conversationally stumbling ways, trying to make things better. May had been cripplingly agoraphobic for three years and our Tommy was gently asking her to come out with both of us into the sunshine, telling her the summer air would do us all the world of good. Of course, May was saying no, that she couldn't go outside, that her nerves couldn't stand it. Our Tommy was constantly reassuring her that, soon as she felt uncomfortable, he'd bring her back in. This exchange went on for some backwarding/forwarding time and the sing-song vocal tenderness between them was nothing like the raging/fighting scenario of the night before. Whatever it was, for now, had lifted and they both knew it. It was lovely witnessing them together like this; almost worth the previous night's storming barney.

Well, you could imagine my surprise when our Tommy said, 'Gerrid, get y'bat 'n' ball lad, we're goin' into the back square for a game of cricket.' What he meant was, me him and me Ma were going to the second bouquet to play *outside*. I couldn't believe it, honest to God, me Ma was seriously going to leave the house! So I fetched my bat 'n' ball and, with his arm protectively around May's shoulder, constantly calming her, they actually left the flat. Our Tommy was doing what I thought impossible. He had got my mother to be in the open air.

It was a short walk to the always less busy back square and we picked up a few friends along the way. Little John and Stephen tagged along and, if memory serves me correctly, a couple of the Day brothers, Danny 'n' Alec. Maybe because it was such an idyllic, breezy, summer afternoon, or because I was clearly part of a miracle, but to see May with my wonky cricket bat and our Tommy bowling with a clutch of giggling kids messing about was remarkably special. May looked visibly nervous but was still trying to be happily part of it all; she even had a go bowling at our Tommy. I could see tiny moments of tentative calm, fleeting seconds of joy, then the anxious, stiffening, tell-tale signs of tension. It was a lovely half hour, the only half hour I clearly remember my mother being outside. My guess is, May must have felt terribly guilty about the night before, as of course did Thomas, so this was their way of openly apologising, making up; an alfresco meeting in the middle. I remember her saying to Thomas, 'I've had enough now, lad. I wanna get back in, y'don't mind do ye?' Without any argument, immediately placing his arm back across her shoulders and with us following duckling-like behind, our Tommy gently led his Ma home. When we got back in, May put the kettle on and said, 'Thomas, 'aven't you forgotten somethin'?' Our Tommy replied *no* and May said, 'Think you 'ave lad. There in the grate – me poker!' Tommy picked it up and seemingly without effort re-bent it back close to its original shape. Although somewhat repaired, it was always a slightly twisted skewwhiff, with me Ma immediately christening it the Devil's poker.

I don't quite know why my last memories of our Thomas are such a mish-mashing collision, but cloudily collide they do. There's his and Angela's engagement party at the Hollywoods' house. A fantastic do, tonnes of people, a real Scouse celebration, with Ian Hollywood and I relishing our roles as running-about, dick-'ead, younger brothers. Fantastic that is, until seeing our Thomas, like something out of a Western, tumbling down the Hollywoods' staircase, obviously fighting somebody and temporarily halting the celebrations. To this day, I've no idea who he was fighting and, with it being a Scouse do, it was quickly sorted out so that partying and, more importantly, the drinking could recommence. I recall our Chris 'n' Paul discussing what might be happening for Thomas's upcoming twenty-second birthday, desperately wishing I could be part of it all. Then there was a strangely fractious, almost surreal moment outside our 6A bit of the landing concerning a cornered rat, with our Tommy trying to get rid of it with a brush and the rat escaping by jumping over his shoulder. It's not so much the rat, but our Thomas's reaction to it; it wasn't good and somehow freaked him out. I clearly remember, because it seriously concerned and troubled May. 'Something's up with him Gerrid,' she told me. 'He wouldn't just be scared of a rat.' That rat story was bleak and became a passed-down/always-told, like some kind of mystically dooming portent. May was dead right though, there was something up. Our Tommy was facing a court case and it was serious. I recall intense family conversations about it. In one of those emotively-charged, family pow-wows, I remember Thomas defiantly and angrily stating, 'There's no fuckin' way I'm goin' to jail, no fuckin' way!'

In the Gerry Marsden film *Ferry Cross the Mersey*, there's a skilfully-crafted, monochromatic scene where Gerry and his Pacemakers are singing in a Liverpool city centre shop window. It's not the hymnal-like, titular anthem, but a fab 'n' gear slice of swinging Merseybeat called 'Baby You're So Good to Me'. A visibly thrilled crowd has gathered outside the window to watch the then hugely famous band and, in that crowd for a precious few seconds, four in fact, you can clearly see Big John and Thomas. Some fine fortuitous day in 1964/5 they were in the right place at the right time and stumbled upon the filming of this movie. A still stubbornly, early-fifties, dark quiff'd-up Big John, alongside a sixteen-/seventeen-year-old, mousy, straight-hair'd Thomas, stood together clearly relishing the moment. Within those precious four seconds the best is when they, without looking to each other, smile at exactly the same time. It's a broadly confident Butler smile, a big brother smile. The smiles I remember every day. I freeze-frame a lot.

VII
The Sons of May Butler: Chris 'n' Paul

Oh man, they were wild and I mean almost feral; their collected energy so rip-roaring raw, haphazardly creative and hyperactively madcap it's impossible with words to in any way recreate. So much of who/what they were autonomous physicality, teen abandon, absurd noises, competitive farting, and hugely-splayed shapes. If anything sticks out, it'd be their shared improvisational fearlessness; always in the bang-of-moment, they shot/rebounded a ricocheting everywhere. Wherever the place, whatever its structure, they were all over it; out loud raucously laughing, their spirits alive with the eclectic musicality of the time. Such the inherently corporeal mystery of their wildly acrobatic skills, they seemed to be able to swing off thin air. Yeah, pretty sure they could fly. Their indefatigably careering wall-shadows certainly did.

Thomas was a laugh, but definitely the authoritative man of the house, looking over things with a bit more adulting seriousness. Of that particular incarnation of family, he was the newest dad. That left me, the youngest, and then my two older brothers, Chris 'n' Paul, as the unruly, troublesome kids. Chris 'n' Paul were far more unruly and troublesome than I ever could be; I didn't have their remarkable, out-there, physical skillsets. I completely adored all my brothers, but remembering these two as young teenagers means I've a more in-the-moment fondness for our Buck 'n' Buck. Buck was bandied about much more than Butch, so if we were all together it was difficult to know which Buck was being spoken to. Those young Bucks though, Chris 'n' Paul Butler... if any of my brothers suited the instantaneous vivacity of that particular headline, it was them. When getting up to no good is what you do every single day (and getting up to no good is what my two older brothers daily did), then as the youngest brother some of that no good is bound to rub off on you. And yes, it did. I accepted the rub, and lo, it was good.

Although worn-down-historically used to it, May hated any shape of trouble coming to the door. She was frightened, threatened by authority; it mentally and physically depleted her. Sadly, trouble-to-the-door shapes were what Chris 'n' Paul often crafted. Especially our Paul.

There was one particularly unforgettable week. May 'n' I had woken up (let's say it's Monday morning) and as everyday-usual she opened the kitchen door. To our stunned surprise the room was, almost from ceiling to floor, filled with fruit and veg. Honestly, it looked like a scene from Alastair Sim's *Scrooge*, the one where a velvety, bloated, bush-bearded Ghost of Christmas Present appears to Ebenezer and has magically festooned the measly miser's bedroom with a Victorian-garlanded Christmas feast. When me Ma asked what all this was about and where did it come from, our Paul confidently told her it was given to him 'n' Chris by someone called Harry, who ran one of the many fruit barrers in town. It was a whole load of excess stuff he didn't need and would soon go off, so he'd insisted they *take it away, lads*.

Tuesday morning came. May 'n' I woke up and again to our surprise the kitchen was once again full. But this time with boxes of baked beans, loads of them everywhere. We were instantly trapped in our own living room, having to squeeze through a maze of giant squares. Some of the boxes were placed on top of each other, avant-garde cubist art resembling huge, Heinz-branded, cardboard steps. When May asked a now warily suspicious *why?*, our Paul explained they were leftovers from a food consignment that couldn't fit onto some lorry by Arden House, so people passing by were told they could bring 'em home.

Wednesday morning dawned and there's now a strangely thick stench; that heady, slightly ugly aroma you might get from a butcher's shop. We walked into the kitchen to be confronted by a reeking, nose-riot of just-murdered slaughter. Raw, reddened meat was everywhere; joints of beef, legs of lamb, half calf ribs, mountainous strings of sausages, pale-skinned just-plucked chickens, and all kinds of fleshy, red/purple offal. It was abattoir awful, a Scottie Road version of *The Texas Chainsaw Massacre*. Once again May asked why and our Paul casually stated that the freezers had conked out in some city centre shops and, again, they were giving all this stuff to whomsoever happened to be nearby. If May was still suspicious, which I'm sure she was, she held it back, because things like this could/did happen. And, to be honest, she took a fair bit of the meat herself to go with the veg she'd snaffled and the many tins of beans.

On the Thursday, when there was no too-sweet scent of fresh veg, no pseudo-artistic, complex hazard of cardboard boxes, no choking clag of purpling flesh, we got up, walked into the kitchen, and everywhere was covered in giant cuddly toys. Mostly teddy bears, with the odd orange/white giraffe and a whole host of other fluffy animals (pretty sure there were googly-eyed owls). Our kitchen looking like an absurd, surrealistic fairyland thrilled me to wide-eyed, jaw-dropped pieces, but May instantly blew her top. 'Right, I gerri' now, I know wha' yous two 'ave been up too, yiv been down the fuckin' docks robbin' again, 'aven't y's!'

They had of course, but our Paul, right in her face, swore to The Sacred Heart above us, that they hadn't. My mother certainly knew something untoward was daily occurring, but when it came to anything to do with kids, especially their toys, it sent her stratospherically ballistic. She must have thought they'd been taken away from them, stolen, and she would never have tolerated anything like that. Screaming blue bloody murder, May chased Chris 'n' Paul out the house, throwing those giant cuddly toys over the landing at them. The memory of a just-flung, giant cuddly giraffe bouncing offa our Paul's back as he's legging it from the block still makes me giggle. Although she could let the veg, beans 'n' meat into the house (after all, we were poor and it was food), me Ma firmly drew the line at cutesy teddies… 'The robbin' bastards, takin' kids' toys away from them like tha', I'm tellin' y'now f'nottin' Gerrid, when I get my 'ands on them their miserable lives won't be worth livin'!' Although May was molten-seething (she was quite the lava-spewing matriarch), have to say they were some of my favourite days in 6A.

When young, our Chris was whippet-lean and just as fast. So skinny, for some strange Scouse reason, May nicknamed him Caveman. The only one of my older brothers with a street-moniker other than Butch or Buck. Of us all, our Caveman seemed to understand most and obey the odd, rickety built, mother/brother hierarchy we had going on. Unlike our Paul, who thought himself an anarchic, untouchable/indestructible king of the world, Chris enjoyed and, more importantly, understood his particular placing within the family make-up. He had a tremendous and clearly visible respect for his older siblings, whilst at the same time being the bossy elder to me and Paul. I think at that impressionable age he was learning from them all, especially Thomas, whom he hero-worshipped.

There's no denying our Chris was a scurrying, ragtag tear-away, but of him 'n' Paul he was by far the most pragmatically creative. He could automatically turn his hand to anything and make something, whatever it was, happen. He was forever building new bikes from old spares and, simply because he wanted to and in a very short space of time, taught himself the mouth organ. A fantastic artist who took the time every day to teach me how to draw. I recall showing him a picture of a girl I drew; probably Andy Pandy's bezzy, Looby Loo. At the extreme ends of her wide, triangular, blue dress, 'n' like young kids do, I had etched her badly crayoned, red-ribbon-shoed legs. Chris outright told me it was wrong and that her legs should be at the centre of the dress, because legs are always part of the bottom half of a body, not where the skirt stops. That simple piece of information was a mind-blowing, artistic revelation to me. The next day I went to school, drew a girl (very probably Looby Loo again; I was obsessed), this time placing her legs where they should anatomically be. The drawing was picked as that week's Best Picture in the Class, a gold-star winner no less. Our clearly impressed teacher even told the class that when drawing legs that was where they should properly go. So, my clever big brother didn't just correctly instruct me; his simple but brilliant advice instantly improved the artistic prowess of my whole classroom.

It was our Chris who helped me make my first steerie (Scouse for 'go-kart'). Well, I say helped. If helped means I just sat and watched him make it, then yes, I helped a great deal. It was on a superbly warm summer's afternoon and all the ingredients needed to make a steerie were practically lying around the square. He must have had some stuff with/on him, tools 'n' such, but there were always sheets of wood and spare wheels thrown out or junked. Our 'oller was chock-a-block with bits of everything; a dumping ground for the unwanted and, in some cases, still usable. My job, how I *helped*, was by collecting them. Christopher Anthony Butler, out of old prams, bits of bikes, hardboard and rope, made my steerie in super speed. It felt like he knocked it up in minutes and, y'know, maybe he did. Warra hotchpotch machine though! It was magnificent, the rickety Rolls Royce of steeries. Largely wooden, with two big pram wheels at its back 'n' two much smaller ones at its head, he'd also fashioned a rope-attached axle mechanism with which you could steer, hence the wildly imaginative descriptor. Every kid, especially lads, had one of these brother/dad street-constructed vehicles and I was more than made up with mine. You were either shoulder-pushed by a mate over whatever slight gradient or taken to the top of a hill, then heftily shoved down.

Very little was ever shop-bought for us and that's not just because of the cost; some families had money. Building, crafting stuff, especially playthings for kids, was simply a handed-down, rights-of-passage moment to communally share and enjoy. The thrilling blast wasn't whether my steerie cost more than your steerie, we didn't have three-striped, gold-plated Adidas steeries; they weren't meant to be in any way competitively designer flash. The gritty, hands-dirty, finger-splintering joy was you could make one from scratch, then same-day play on it. I holistically adored every ramshackle inch of my Caveman-built steerie.

It's also worth noting that our Chris's go-carting invention finally took away the unforgiving rage I'd built up over that crap fuckin' scooter me Ma had got me. Hey, who knows, maybe its front little wheels were from that ridiculously awkward looking contraption. I most sincerely hope so. Near-sleekly-designed, wobbly-four-wheeled poetic justice at last!

After age fifteen, education back then, for what it was worth, was brutally taken from you, but it didn't stop thousands of employers needing their yearly dose of just-left-school factory fodder. Of course, that wasn't fair, especially when, like my brother, you were a naturally-gifted, educationally-unrealised creative. Societal structures were far more employment-fixed, but that did mean some people were socially/financially freer and able to join in with the world around them. Our Chris knew this and delighted in having a firm and valued place in those secure industrial landscapes. Yes, he worked the factory daily, but by the end of week (and especially with overtime) he was a gregariously outgoing teenager/young adult with a fat wad of just-earned spondoolies to spend on whatever/whoever he wanted and however/wherever he liked.

Bone-marrow-embedded in Chris Butler was a proud Vauxhall/Scottie Road take-no-bullshit attitude which he'd take everywhere with him. Poverty or pay didn't shut any of us up, the opposite being the case. We were not from that drearily clichéd *nowhere/nothing* celebrities with too much money and no brains, who make even more money and still with no brains, bemoan. We were most definitely people from *somewhere* who knew stuff. More importantly, these *someones* would confidently 'n' proudly tell you exactly where that *somewhere* was; that place *definitely* being Blackstock Gardens.

Being eighteen months older than Paul, our Chris did that magically transformative thing before him. One day he was a hungry-eyed, getting into all kinds of trouble, knockabout, caveman-esque teenager, next, yer actual full grown working man. Leaving school and getting a job did that. At the same time, he quickly, athletically, filled out, suddenly looking in fantastic, masculine shape. Whatever had been skinny-kid-Neanderthal of-the-street about him seemingly overnight vanished. In one superhuman leap 'n' bound there he magnificently was, just like our Thomas, togged-up in posh/flash weekending clobber. We were always a good-looking family, but something extra hand-some seemed to happen to our Chris; he became a fantastically attractive young man and knew it… Christ, did he know it!

Our Chris garnered a lot of female attention, that's for sure, some of whom he'd night-time bring back to 6A. May let the lads do what they did because she thought it better than a drunken knee-trembler down a smelly enog (Scouse for 'back entry'/'jigger'). For all her long-baked Catholicism and high-strung temperament, at times May was quite a modern-day free-thinker.

It was at this point in my young life that I was often left wondering why so many girls were called Judy. I loved my MGM Judy Garland, but instinctively knew she wasn't the reason so many mothers called their daughters after her. Also, everybody I knew in the sixties was Catholic, meaning you had to be named after a saint, and to my knowledge there was certainly no St. Judy. Believe me, I'd have known if there was ever a St. Judy, Patron Saint of Uppers 'n' Downers. So, how could it be then, that every girl was suddenly called that? Judy, it transpired, was a colloquial, slang term that boys/men used for girls or potential girlfriends. For our lads, Judy as a girl's name seemed to become incredibly popular when hitting puberty and getting a job: *Arr 'ey kid, shoulda seen the kip of the Judy I copped for last night, fuckin' gear-lookin'!* There were lots of girls, all of them seemingly gear-looking, and every one mysteriously called Judy. I remember thinking, that when older, and even if their names weren't Judy, was I was gonna have to call all girls Judy as well? It's safe to say that didn't happen. The only Judys I called Judy were Judys whose only names were Judy.

After those hundreds of Judys, our Chris's male mates all seemed to genuinely be called Tommy. No, it wasn't a puberty-induced, nicknaming affectation; there was Tommy Arnek, Tommy Malone 'n' Tommy McMahon. He had lots of other mates, but probably because of brother Tommy, they stuck out to me most. What a brilliant bunch of Tommys they were. Every Friday payday they'd pile into 6A, all of them making a pun-jibing fuss of May, and she loved it. When surrounded by handsome, fit, young men, my middle-aged mother could turn into quite the flirting call girl. They'd somehow hurl me round like a ball, catching me in their arms or on their shoulders, often spinning me round like a marching band baton or magician's plate. Then, once again, the beer-drinking ribbing 'n' joking at each other's incredibly good-looking expense, until they all but boogied out of the door. You could hear their hysterical laughter fading as they walked along the landing to the stairs. I'd tiptoe to peer over at them leaving our stairwell below. Watching as they near-jived across the square, I'd smile-wide marvel at their obvious kinship and freeing physicalities. As a child, I found their undiluted brio and fun-loving fervour overwhelmingly intoxicating. After they'd gone, my energy levels would be so hyperactively high that I'd be metaphysically left wanting on the ceiling. There I'd be, next to our torn, frilled lampshade, peering down at our grubby lino and at the top of May's roots-greying head, longing to be going with them to that mythical place called *town*… and one day dammit, I will!

Being the next youngest, our Paul, on occasion, might have to über-reluctantly babysit me. May would have probably been out at the bingo with her bezzy Annie King, leaving me in the not-so-loving charge of my angrily sulking older brother. I say older brother (he had ten years on me), but he was more a loud-mouthed, pugnacious bruiser. I'm now completely convinced our Paul was the first scally. I vividly recall hanging around him and his two mates, Gerry Marsden and Robbie Orr. I'd spend quite a bit of time with them out in the square and Paul hated, nay, absolutely loathed, me tagging along. Paul Butler wasn't what you'd call a natural babysitter; he was certainly no Mary Poppins, his style of sibling nurturing being something a bit rougher, readier and more hands-on feral than, say, other experienced child minders or mythical nannies. Instead of cheerily sing-song administering a spoonful of sugar to help the medicine go down, he would literally treat me and pick me up like a yelping wolf cub.

I was always dead impressed by his mate Gerry because of his shared surname with Gerry of Gerry and the Pacemakers fame. I must have nightly, right royally, pissed him off every time I'd say, 'Aye Gerry, are you Gerry off the telly; are you Gerry an' the Pacemakers' Gerry?' Thing is, he had that same shortish black hair and cheeky bravado, but that was about it;

he clearly wasn't the lead singer of Liverpool's second biggest band. I must have thought it completely hysterical to keep telling him that one thing over 'n' over. Gerry was a great guy and calmly patient with me, unlike our Paul who'd yell, 'Warra ya fuckin' onnabout Gerrid, y'tit-'ead, of course he's not Gerry from Gerry an' the fuckin' Pacemakers, the real Gerry Marsden's Gerry from Gerry an' the Pacemakers, not this Gerry… y'embarrassin' me an' yerself, now shut it dick-'ead, schnell!' So, of course, I'd say, 'Is our Paul right then Gerry, so you're not Gerry from Gerry an' the Pacemakers?' Paul Butler always seemed to be in a perpetual state of wanting to strangle me. With a vibrant tussle of electrically enthused curly hair framing his film-star handsome face, Robbie Orr was also dead funny. Robbie was slightly quieter than the other two, but tremendously one-liner witty; nothing passed by his sharp, caustic eye.

Being a tinny-voiced nuisance and hanging around our Paul was boss, la. The greatest thing about being babysat by my next oldest brother was you got to see what he night-times got up to. If lucky, you might even have sometimes had a proactive role in it; your job being to keep dixie. Dixie was looking out for the police or whether anyone in authority, let's say from the docks, might be tramping around. I'll leave the rest to your lively imaginations. Have to say though, I was a fantastic dixie keeper.

All this would have occurred before May's agoraphobia took hold, because I again remember being out really late. It's all so murky, more recalling the visceral thrill of it happening rather than the structural narratives of occasion, but here we go…

On this particular night, our Paul wasn't with his normal mates, but was once again, and under much sibling duress, looking after me. I've still no idea who the other guy was, but for some odd reason we were off the street and almost instantly inside a car. Odd, because it wasn't our car; we didn't own one. I'm a fidgeting inquisitive in the back of this crate, looking at the two in the front who seemed to be messing around with where the handbrake might be. Now, I'm not sure hotwiring was a thing then and they may have had a makeshift key device, but whatever they were frantically doing to get this vehicle moving did indeed work. Our Paul started to drive and, such the force of take-off, I was thrown into the back of my seat. Soon as that happened, we were screeching incredibly fast into the night. I was face-to-the-window, thrilled to bits by all this, thinking everything was okay and our Paul must just be driving his mate in the front's car; after all, he was fourteen. I loved it! We were speeding around/about so fast 'n' there were so many blurring, coloured lights; it was like being a single bead in an ADHD-diagnosed kaleidoscope. We tore up Scottie Road and must have got onto Blackstock Street, heading for Vauxhall Road, when behind us we heard a sirens-wailing panda car. There was a series of laughing/panicking *fuckin' 'ell!*s from the two in the front, and then I'm re-thrown into the back of the seat as the now road-swerving car skid-screeched to a vehicle-curving halt. Our Paul dived out and super-humanly threw me from of the back of the motor onto the street, away from it/them. He 'n' his mate then legged it to a sheer, red brick wall, one-climb scaled it and got away. They didn't have a Bat-rope or anything and literally scampered up that wall like spider-men. I've no real idea why the police didn't get me, but suddenly, somehow, I found myself in the safe hands of the Kings, Annie's daughters – ironically, my usual babysitters. It does sound terribly dangerous and, of course, don't try this at home folks, but it was so much fun. I can't remember the commotion afterwards, but there must have been some, and it may have something to do with what would shortly happen to Paul. On the whole though, it was just another evening being baby-sat in the everyday lives of my baby-sitters every-night-living-it.

Our Paul was always in trouble with someone, something, or the law; in many ways, couldn't help himself. He needed a lot happening around him and on the surface seemed to be able to skilfully, gleefully juggle chaos. He would have been ten when Jimmy Butler left my mother and I remember her saying that, although always a bit of wild one, he got a lot wilder and more uncontrollable when his dad had gone. May would have been a clearly-wrecked heartbroken about all of that and then, all of a sudden, out I popped. Not only was our Paul emotionally in bits by the abandonment of his father, now his increasingly problematic mother had a new baby to over-devote herself to. There was no other way for him to go. The rails, although always a wobbly-warped, were now no way negotiable; the only logical trajectory being off them. In a family of already quite discoloured sheep, our Paul became the most discoloured.

There was real, heart-pumping commotion going on in 6A; something was well and truly up. It was all atmospherically jagged and our Paul, a frantically-startled jittery. May 'n' our Chris were trying to calm him down but to no avail. Nothing about calming appeasement was ever going to land, whatever was going on had unsettled everything.

I suddenly became aware that our Paul was this nervous because the police were coming to arrest him. It might well have been for the stolen car we joy-rode in, but who knew – it really could've been anything. Paul Butler was bang-into nickin' lead off roofs, particularly churches; there was a lot of money in lead 'n' copper piping, so perhaps there was a few bob extra if it was holy. Whatever the police had on him, without any doubt, was going to stick. Also, our Paul was the spitting image of evidence.

Once again, the ominous whine of sirens; a Blackstock Gardens aural calling card. Lots of young men in our tenement got into trouble, so when the police came a-wooing, they were greeted by a whole range of its residents. Some on the landings, women with babes in arms, looking, shouting down, and some were lads, men even, circling the panda car, clearly two-finger signalling that the police weren't welcome.

In 6A it was a lot like that Jimmy Cagney movie, *Angels with Dirty Faces*, as our Paul, finally pulling himself together, slowly became resigned to his cellblock fate. Head high, shoulders back, he began to leave the house to greet the coppers. He'd been gone less than a minute when I completely lost it; there was no way they were going to take my brother away from me. Screaming his name, I ran along the landing, down the stairs and across to the square where the panda was parked. All I panicking remember was our Paul's concerned face at the police car window, his angry index finger thumping the glass, telling me to get the fuck back in. I wasn't having any of it; I was repeatedly fist-banging the panda, demanding they let him out. As the motor sped away, I ran after it, continually bawling my brother's name. Concern erupted with people in the square and, after being cared for by everybody 'n' still hopelessly sobbing, I walked a limping, weeping wounded home. I wasn't sure what had really gone on. It was all so surreal feeling and teary blurry, but I convinced myself I'd never see my brother again. I was a dramatically-crumpled bereft when getting back in and he wasn't there, collapsing on our couch like an exhausted Theda Bara. I could palpably feel it. I was only five/six years old and 6A wasn't the same any-more. There was one less shadow on its wall, meaning one of my beloved brothers had gone.

Approved school was great. Well, it was for me. Not that I ever got to attend, but our Paul did, and was in and out for a while. It was a long bus drive which I loved, with our Thomas or Chris whom I also loved; what more could I ask for? It would have mostly been with Chris, who seemed to psychically know exactly what to get our Paul and, more intriguingly, knew how to secretly pass it to him. Again, it never felt dangerous or oppressive; in fact, I found it all an interestedly exciting. It was more than great to see our Paul and there was something about how you had to sit opposite each other, whilst being watched over, that made me think I was in some kind of gangster movie. This must have been a longer stay for my next youngest brother because, suddenly on one visit, he seemed to be older. He'd always looked like a youthful, just-punched cushion, but he was adulting now, changing. He was doing that exact same thing our Chris had been doing and had, by now, done… he was becoming a man.

The directionless, shapeless scally, who reluctantly went into approved school, came out a lean, fit young bloke and, naturally, there was a party. Our Paul had changed: he wasn't that reckless kid in the stolen car and no longer had to attend ordinary school; he too could work for a weekly wage. My brothers, once finding manual labouring work, all but ceased their once nefarious night-time activities. There were no more criminally light-footed, moonlit trips to the docks for me. Except on certain occasions with our Paul.

Chris 'n' Paul had been teen coalmen on Bert's coal-wagon. I remember it well because my nephew Little John and I would often be able to tag along. I think all my brothers at some time worked for Bert the coalman. It must have been summer because, soon as the sun came out, these now buff, be-muscled couple of Bucks would be boastfully showing off their taught, ripped, covered in coal-soot torsos.

One fine day, Bert's coal-wagon was parked by our part of the tenement. Bert, his coalmen, with big, black, hessian sacks over their shoulders, were door-to-door delivering their shiny, anthracitic wares, leaving me and Little John sat in the coal-wagon's cabin. Because we were kids and getting fidgety bored, I started looking for something else to do other than sit quietly. This might've been a hangover from my recent car-robbing past, but for some reason I decided to turn the key of the ignition. I also must've known to take the handbrake off, making the coal-wagon rev into life and start to move forward – we were now heading straight towards a couple of ground-floor flats. Little John was a bit nervous and I was a kind of jumping-up-'n'-down overjoyed. No sooner had I put my tiny hands on the giant steering wheel in order to somehow drive the thing, than our Paul had ripped open the coal-wagon's door, athletically dived in, pushed me away from the wheel and, just in the nick, stopped this enormous wagon from colliding into someone's front wall. I immediately knew I'd done something monstrously wrong when, by the scruff of my neck, I was violently dragged out the cabin and given an almighty telling off from my raging big brothers. They were scarlet-faced furious with me so I probably got a belt off them to. More than just angry; they were concerned I may have damaged myself and Little John. Unlike Little John, and to my absolute fury, I was banned from going into the coal-wagon ever again. It would break my heart to see Little John way up in the lorry looking down at me, probably laughing because I was no longer allowed in.

It's dawning on me more 'n' more writing this just what a little terror I was, and here's me thinking I was good as gold, the quiet one. It was also around about that time our Paul had to kick down our locked bathroom door because I'd set fire to the *Liverpool Echo* toilet paper, which then set alight the peeling wallpaper above the lav. Probably got a belt for that too. Even effetely MGM-musical-centric as I was, like my brothers 'n' mother, I was just as serially bloody-minded. If wanting to do something, I'd find a way to do it. Shouting at me never worked, nor did the rare back-hander. It's like I've always said... never underestimate the effeminate child, or he might just crash a coal-wagon into your back-kitchen or burn down your bog!

Our Chris 'n' Paul were quite simply the best older siblings any younger sibling could have. They weren't always easy on me; sometimes I'd get a good telling off and a clip around the ear-'ole, but they loved me the way only big brothers can. I could have done without being pinned down on the floor so one them could squat on my face and fart in it though. Yeah, that properly pissed me off. That, and the furious tickling till I cried, loudly insisting I submit, whatever that meant. Hanging me over the landing 'n' telling me they were gonna drop me wasn't a bag of laughs either. They weren't ever only that though; aside from the endless, seemingly hysterically funny farting tricks, I felt completely and holistically protected by them. They looked out for and after me.

On payday/pocket money Fridays our Chris loved taking me into town. Being a now-seasoned-townie, he knew lots of people and liked to show off his new clothes – clothes he'd ask my opinion of. God, I loved it when he'd do that. It made me feel I had a proactive role in how he so brilliantly looked... now that's teaching! We'd spend some time in a couple of his favourite townie pubs, those big-bloke, city centre boozers feeling to tiny me like too-loud, joyful museums. There was just so much brightly chatted conversational laughter in the air, instantly lifting your spirits the way the best music does. Afternoon drinkers and drinking seemed somewhat different to its much wilder night-time counterpart; much more footballing-tribally male. He was showing what life would or could be like for me and I relished it. Be it for a silly trick, stink bombs, a horror mask, luminous paint, fake poo or fireworks, I adored going into The Wizard's Den with him, a joke shop nearby in town. Just walking into that densely atmospheric magician's cave with my protective big brother made everything in the world seem right. He could clearly see the open-faced, smiling joy of me simply being in there and would be broad-beaming right back at me. If I was happy so was he.

Our Paul was almost the opposite, definitely an adult, but a big kid too. He never grew up, not because he couldn't; he simply never wanted to. He was a fantasist, a dreamer, endlessly energised, full of anarchic plotting and world domination. He was both a high-flying Peter Pan and mercurial

Pied Piper. On pocket money days he'd buy loadsa sweets for the kids living nearby and, as they'd cheeringly gather around him, he'd generously dish them out. Like Big John, Paul, in both mental attitude and physical demeanour, possessed that instinctive partying spark. He also loved being centre of attention and could confidently be it, carrying it off with characterfully upbeat, ringmaster aplomb. Put him in any tricksy position/situation and he'd get out of it, or at least try to. A circus escapologist without ropes or chains, possessing all the vivacious sparkling aura of that top-hatted, whip-cracking, crowd-controlling showmanship. Blackstock Gardens' very own car, lead, copper-pipe, water-tank robbin' Houdini. He loved kids, especially family, and was the brother/uncle/cousin who had us all hysterically piling on top of him. He was a spark igniting the fuse, sizzling its fizzing way toward the powder kegs.

Like disparately placed fireworks in a rusting old biscuit tin, we familiarly lay. Our Jimmy was without doubt a fearlessly exploding, energetically unafraid banger. Big John, an effervescing, comedically colour-shooting roman candle. Our Thomas, a fashionably classy, subtly dynamic, flare-trailing rocket. Our Chris, the blurring, creatively spiralling circles of a catherine wheel. Our Paul, a trickster-informed, jump-jigging rip-rap. May? That's simple: a molten-lava-spewing, mood-changing, spark-spitting Mount Vesuvius. Me? Well, one day I'd glow up to be a chrysanthemum cascade, but back then I was, and happy to be, a prissy little sparkler.

VIII
Bommy Night

In *Meet Me in St. Louis*, the Vincente Minnelli-directed MGM musical starring Judy Garland and Margaret O'Brien, there's a large cast of colourful characters, but none of them bigger or more important than where they live. In fact, the Smiths' salmon-pink mansion becomes the central heart of its schmaltzy plot; another protagonist. I felt and still feel like that about Blackstock Gardens. So much went on around/about Blackie, but when it came to high drama and comedy, that broad-shouldered, lantern-jawed tenement, like Garland, always had its name above the title. I adored how Minnelli romantically picture-framed the palatial house the Smith family sing-song inhabited. Every turn of season gives off a differing elemental, almost ephemeral sense of where and how they existed. Ornately lid-of-chocolate-box illustrated, a familial, saccharine fantasy; their elegantly velvet-draped home organically changing within the surrounding year. Winter; white/blue snowy covered, red-ribbon wrapped and hands-on home-made Christmassy. Spring; a blossom-budding, eventually-blooming lush pastel blush, a vaudevillian *you-like-a-me like-I-like-a-you*, skirts-lifting, petticoating gay. Summer; densely green and full-flowering, as an eternally optimistic New England sun shines down on boy-next-door flirting, hands-held circling, knee-dipping jigs. Fall; fruit-bruised autumnal, leaf-crunching tawny, fulsomely pumpkin-orange and exquisitely bathed in the raggedy-clad, mischievous trickeries of the month. Okay, so it wasn't set in the luxuriant opulence of late nineteenth century America; we were a crumbling, thirties, dockland tenement, slap-bang in the middle of more polluting industry than you could shake a shitty stick at. But, like the all-singing/dancing *ding ding ding went the bell* flurry of a trolley-sung, Hollywood-built St. Louis, Liverpool's Blackstock Gardens also mythically changed with the seasons.

Duck Apple Night or, if you prefer, Halloween, was a wonderfully freeing affair. Being surrounded by the shadowing enormities of where we lived gave this traditionally spooky night a more mysterious, literary/filmic feel. Behind any of its doors, a silver candelabra-lit Bram Stoker, quill dipping in recently slaughtered virgin blood, could furiously be scribbling out another vampiric classic. In the autumnal thrall of those late October landings, every tall, cavernous gap looked a liminally-imposing, Christopher-Lee-shaped gateway. Being brought up on horror movies, double-bills of late-night TV terror called *Appointment with Fear*, we completely got and literally ran with that. I was as comfortable with snarling werewolves and lumbering, reanimated cadavers as I was with the rhyming, pinpoint accuracies of Two-balls and the song-sung athleticisms of skipping. We didn't spend any cash on Duck Apple (maybe we might have got bought or gotten hold of a couple of scary rubber masks from The Wizard's Den), but it was nowhere near as brightly partying as it is now. We presided over a more organic, darkened, storytelling Halloween, not a door-to-door-sweets-collecting holiday.

One Duck Apple, May burnt the end of a cork on our coal fire and, using it to smear curling, black streaks all over our faces, she painted us evil. The curving sweeps of inky kohl markings highlighting our eyes, mouths and cheeks, instantly turned us into knee-crouching, claws-up demons; I thought it actual witchcraft. Annie King was always up to a minxy something, but especially so on this tricksy night. For a scary jape, she'd pop out the top set of her false teeth onto the edge of her bottom lip and, hiss-cackling away, declare herself a witch. Then, by boiling alive in a big black pot on her back-kitchen stove, she'd threaten to gobble up any kids passing her gate. When it came to terrifying the crap out of children, this über-glamorous woman had no surface vanity whatsoever. With her wicked witch falsies flap-snapping from a gummy crone-crowing gob, she especially put the shits up our Stephen. Till this day, a visibly shaken Stephen Butler cites that as one of the scariest moments of his childhood. Believe me, you only get one Annie King; how I wish there were more.

Duck Apple Night belonged to us kids but, like everything, adults would be in on it too. It'd be in Big John and Mary Mac's flat where we'd snap and duck apple. How much fun is it trying to blindfolded mouth-grab a line of strung-up golden delicious or cox pippins, then, with hyper-giggling heads-bumping urgency, try to bite them from a bowl of freezing water? All the fun in the world, that's how much, and made all the more hilarious with Big John joining in. My funny older brother was a bigger, happier, partying kid than any of us; every move he made a flurrying, musical reel. There was a giggling improvisational vibe to those festivities, feeling like the best thing that could possibly be happening. Add to that the head-spinning giddiness o' the thru'penny bits and tanners secretly embedded within those apples, not only were we laughing our tiny heads off, but we were suddenly tooth-chipped, corner shop rich. Not sure we were told too much about Halloween and for the life of me I can't remember how its information was passed down; but like everything about everything, there was a communal osmosis in how we were gifted knowledge.

Later, sitting outside on darkened stairwell steps with hollowed-out, candle-lit, scary-faced turnips under our chins, we'd tell each other ghost stories. Didn't matter that those grey stone stairs were freezing; in fact, frozen arses atmospherically added to the moment. Fogged within acrid stench of burning swede, it was all about deliberately spooking the undead horrors out of each other. There were many passed down, regularly told, spine-chilling tales, so it was dead easy to own, distort and retell them... Local ghost stories of a bloodied, be-fanged, roof-leaping, fire-breathing Spring Heeled Jack... With his green, pallid face and ghastly agonising wail, shimmering away in his abandoned first-floor flat, the lonely spirit of old Mr Lee... We left no Victorian vampire buried and blasphemy-like thrilled in bringing recently deceased neighbours back to mythically scary life. In front of a black/blue-framed full moon, the Devil's Eye, Little John and I swore we could see a coven of broomstick-skriking witches cackle past. To this day, I'm not sure we didn't. Through all of that excitably stuttered tale-spilling there was this oddly comforting feeling we were being held in the monstrous red brick claw of our tenement. It seemed to want huddle closer into us, to be let in on the nightmarish spooks we were sneakily resurrecting.

In the repetitively drilling chaos of my pneumatically strobing head, Blackie's always there, towering over, listening, forever knowing, and even seasonally monstrously-garbed, loyally protecting.

There's a wonderful, almost touch-tangible moment in *Meet Me in St. Louis* (my favourite in fact), where Margaret O'Brien's Tootie, along with her young friends and sister, go turn-of-the-twentieth-century trick or treating. Oh, the colours, costumes and textures of those scenes; even monochrome flickering they reach out, almost caressing your skin. A wide-eyed Tootie, although frightened, is dared by her motley gang to go to the Braukoffs' house and kill! To do so, she must hurl a murderous bag of flour at them. Beautifully acted by a precociously talented O'Brien, Tootie step-by-step edges down a darkened path and ever closer to the Braukoffs' ungodly door. Egged on by her more fearful, slightly older cohorts, she's urged to throw her deadly flour bomb into the elderly couple's faces. This little girl, with all the snaggle-toothed, tremble-lip'd courage she can muster, bravely screams *I hate you, Mr Braukoff!*, flour-bomb-walloping the smiling old man right into his startled kisser. Elated by their tiny pal's indomitable courage and perfect aim, the rest of these miniature ghouls screech out my favourite line in the movie: *Tootie killed the Braukoffs!*.

Now, we didn't ever do it like little Miss Smith; it seemed Tootie was even more wickedly scally than we were. We didn't go from door-to-door with homemade, self-raising explosives, desperate to fatally wound lovely Mrs Dreah. Who in their right mind would want to mercilessly blow up a kindly old woman? Oh no, we were saving our more murderous energies for the star of the show, the main attraction. In five nights' time the next act would blow Duck Apple Night completely off the stage. We never thought killing our benign 'n' sharing neighbours a thing to festively make happen, but, sure as hell savages the dammed, we were gonna maniacally torture seven kinds of fright out of Bonfire Night.

Bommy Night, as I've always known/called it, was uniquely special. I loved it way back then and still madly in love with it now. Its historically-flaring anarchies and malformed tellings/retellings continually thrill. The scorched, well-hung-drawn-'n'-quartered stretch of its hellfiring-on-all-cylinders blasts eternally excite. More than anything though, I love it dangerously belongs to children. Yeah, y'heard me, DANGEROULSY! I was one of those children and it was deliciously, dangerously, mine. Dusk-time bommy-wood-robbing from neighbouring tenements' hidden stores was a rough 'n' ready, hard-knock, tribal given. Yes, even I was a tiny, insult-hurling, stone-throwing toddler brave-heart, territorially fighting to protect Blackie's bommy wood from another square's night-time thievery. Dustbin lids as shields 'n' a gob full of just-learnt swearwords, engined-on by a full-throttle battlefield mentality... oh, we were mucky warriors.

The over-excited buying of bangers and rip-raps from The Wizard's Den was what older brothers were perfectly for. Once, for a dare, I let a banger go off in my hand. Yeah, girly ol' me. The proper lads were egging me on, but never expected this high-pitched li'l sissy to truly do it. But do, I damn well did. It was inexcusably dangerous, something no one in their right mind should ever have done, but it felt fuckin' fabulous when that hissing mini bomb didn't blow a finger off. For a brief moment I became the unlikely brave one – bravery so shockingly pronounced it quickly shut up the surrounding scally doubters. For a few precious minutes time stood still and, for a couple of empowering hours, I, queggy, girlygoo Butch Butler, was the hardest of our gang. Yeah, it scorched my thumb, burnt it real bad, but the agony of that black flare-burn was more than worth it. Evil flour bombs my pert Scouse tenement ass! Go swivel on that Tootie Smith! And all the time manifesting, weighing down our shoulders, scorching our necks, tingling our skin, the descending, incendiary delights of Bommy Night.

Long before the 5th, flame-smouldering scents permeated everything, as if time itself were singeing. From several days/nights before, began the peripatetic building of many small fires, whilst at the same time erecting our big bommy. We'd stand around those tiny fires, completely unbothered by the pitter-patterlings of October/November rains; far too busy rubbing chapped-splintered hands on short-trouser'd arses, tin-foil baking our Mas' precious King Edwards in their glowing embers to be bothered by stupid autumnal showers. Neighbours would haul out old furniture to burn, anything from bed-heads to radiograms. There was no end of warped-mirrored wardrobes, tatty three-piece suites and smelly, piss-stained mattresses. Helping them along with all this now unwanted treasure, we'd noisily scrape it to the centre of the square. Semi-circled around it all, we would wide-legged, hands-on-hips, little-man-stanced, proudly witness our bommy grow into a mesmerising, mismatching timber mountain of differing woods and now homeless furnishings. Ours was a many-ringed, auld-oaken community of over-shared familial histories, collectively knowing all that bark; those long-paid-for bites, all this years-soiled furniture, used to be our families'/neighbours' past future debts.

The Woodie (a local timber merchant's) stored impossibly long planks of wood, so over many consecutive nights, we'd sneak under its gates to steal them. After that, the liberation of even more wood from the increasingly emptying, deteriorating flats. Before the unforgivable brutalities of its oncoming demolition, our tenements, homes 'n' communities were brick by brick being systematically ripped apart. Not just by a culturally short-sighted city council, but by our Paul. Athletically swinging from flat to flat, beam to beam, sinewy brave and preternaturally strong, leaping from window to window like a dead-'ard pixie, a scally Puck, our Paul, like our Chris before him, was King of the Bommy. From those empty flats, he and his mates would, through long-smashed-in windows, throw out what had been left abandoned in them. There'd be a choral, hands-in-the-air kid-cheer as old dressing-tables went crashing down, smashing to smithereens on the ground. There was never a prouder little brother. One day I was gonna inherit those superpowers of his and become our Paul.

I'd have ages ago made a guy from my brothers' old jeans 'n' jumpers and painstakingly-detailed drawn a smile-sneering, goateed mask. Then, before the big night, I'd go *on the guy*, pennies-begging with friends or sometimes on my own. To be honest, preferred it alone; felt freer to soak in the increasingly sizzling atmosphere. Pub-corner-stood 'n' smoky bacon toasty, I'd ghost out mouth-cold mists, watching my just-breathed breath-phantoms cloud around white-star electric nights. Stood as if becoming possessed, because I was about to be possessed, *furiously possessed*, my eyes 'n' ears reacting to every flashing, thunderous sound. People were always generous, giving me money or crisps, treacle/cinder-toffee, even toffee apples (fuckin' love toffee apples). In the cloaking shadow of our red brick arch, counting out my just-acquired cash, I'd be side-eyed-neighbour clocked. They'd smile an old smile, I'd a young smile back. All of us were staying out longer than normally allowed, ignoring our Mas' square-searching squalls and kinda secretly gloating. We instinctively knew we were leaving their pinny-strings, their cows, cocks 'n' onions, slapping palms, and many sides.

The Machiavellian visage of a grinning Guy Fawkes, scheme-shady manipulative on the lid of my Standard Fireworks box, was my first hero; still is a hero. Perhaps being such a strong Catholic, left-wing community, poor old Guy wasn't seen as the wicked super-villain our history books cruelly painted him out to be. He was more like our bezzy-mate, our very own bearded, historical, politically-bullied revolutionary. *But tonight, Mr Fawkes, we're the plotting anarchists, the fire-makers 'n' world-shakers… only this time we'll succeed.* I'd gently take my fireworks from their box and count every one, placing them carefully on my bedspread, counting them, counting them, then counting them again. Tiny bright soldiers, all dolled-up for a top-secret inspection; catherine wheels, rockets, witches' cauldrons, roman candles, rip-raps, bangers 'n' sparklers. These weren't just my private tubular militia, but soon-to-be biscuit-tin-hidden gems. Tiny, insurrectionist bombs, jam-packed with rubies, diamonds 'n' sapphires, prepped to shatter into millions more precious stones. Sniffing the box for a quick gunpowder fix, I'd remember, remember the 5th.

It was magic. The pure, undiluted magic of knowing that your whole community was thrilling to their children's first-time reactions to fireworks; a darkening night's rites of back-alleying passages. A huge, volcanic party monster's slowly manifesting. We could feel its feet stomp nearer, its rumbling booming bass, heart-pounding ever closer. Completely welcom-ing this mind 'n' body assimilation, being open-armed corrupted and full-on fire 'n' brimstone dominated, our possession was finally complete. Us, our bodies, our imaginations suddenly and miraculously conjoined, our tiny, bone-rattling bodybags a deep-pumping, lava-flowing florescent.

…A tightly folded *Liverpool Echo* expectantly torches and, from underneath, our mountainous bonfire is lit. A humble smouldering ignites into eventual flare and its fast-growing blaze roars upward. We madly circle around it, giggling, whooping and throwing on more planks of wood, sometimes whole doors. Spraying out such white-hot blasts of blazing wildfire, we hysterically dash from its huge, sparking showers… SCRAM!

Hades, hell for God's sake, its bloody Technicolor self, its unending conflagration, volcanically bursts through our blistering/bubbling tarmacadam about to engulf the tenement – Blackstock Street, Paul Street, Vauxhall Road, Scottie Road, Liverpool, England, the entire fuckin' planet (told you Beelzebub lived under our first bouquet, didn't I!). We throw my guy onto the top of the bommy, laughing at him as he limp 'n' bumbling burns. His lolloping head falls off and an on-fire football tumbles down like a rubbish comet, the bearded mask I so lovingly sketched now long ash'd. That poor, beleaguered, *Liverpool-Echo/Daily-Mirror*-stuffed dummy, recently earning all that lovely lolly outside Cons, my very own collapsed, baggy, villainously Catholic alcoholic, now just another apologetically-scorched, newly-incinerated loser. From long sprawls of landings, pointing down, baby-holding mothers are all in on this supreme act of fiery insurgence. Windows are hot, getting hotter and near cracking. Wretched, bleak and clawing, flaming rubber tyres belch out ever-thickening, poisonous black mists. I'm told there could smog monsters lurking in those murks. Oh, there are monsters alright, brilliant monsters.

Looking into the roar of our hand-crafted perdition and visions of other peoples' hell-spawned Bommy Nights are clearly illustrated. In golden, red, plumes of fiery blur, we see images of our ancestors and they are wildly dancing, demonic furies. We know we're adding to those pictures; know one day we'll be seen, and we'd fury 'n' flail within the flames. Who needs stupid words? This hallucinatory madness is about bathing in and becoming the past, present and future of spectacle.

All my family and I are collected outside 6A. Even May's secretly hovering around the back of her front door, tentatively peeping around at our spectacular fire. The light of bonfire hits, warming our faces, and everybody looks so smiling-gorgeous. Raging flame does that. It glows you up, making you look like you're stood in an oil painting. My brothers, as always, have bought more fireworks than needed, so Little John, Stephen and I, like frenzied, blue-arsed flies, constantly buzz up 'n' down our stairs. After lighting yet another dormant squib on the landing and big-smile watching it crackle, sputter 'n' shine, like speeding kamikaze bluebottles to a butcher's shop insect-o-cuter, we seriously need to be near the bommy.

We've all of us the same feeling of being from spark-spitting/ flame-throwing Liverpool. One for all and all for one of us powerfully stood around our bommy, watching the burning heart of all we are dominate a pitch-blackened sky. This bommy's so damn big the electric light high over the square's burst 'n' its flimsy wire's completely melted. Heat, searing and dangerous, heads beyond our now shattered street-lamp, above our towering tenement towards an already smoke-smothered moon.

From the corner of my eye, I blimp our head-scarf'd, flat-cap'd, wrinkle-faced ancients. They're crumple-huddled in their stairwells scowling out a glum, post-war resistance. Disgruntled, toothless mouths, lip-mumble they're not respons-ible, not to blame, that this on-fire madness was all the bleedin' kids' fault. They're hissing absolute bollocks and know it: it's their radiograms, wardrobes, couches, splitting mirrors, their piss-stained mattresses, barks, bites, their dark-nights-of-the-soul memories going up in flames. It's those old furnishings of theirs housing the furies.

The wailing, pee-pawing of authority comes ever closer and, from a distant whine to a howling halt, they're here. Genuinely, nothing got our backs up quicker than the emergence of the fire-brigade. I was always in mouth-gawping awe of fire engines, especially the ones with those big wheels and ladders; think I kinda fancied them. Not sexually fancied, but there was deffo some sort of *other* human/metal inter-species attraction goin' on. Such flat-/snub-nosed, handsome cabins – like bright red, really fit, punch-drunk boxers; I thought that if they could talk they'd sound like they'd just come out of the ring. However fondly/oddly I felt about them though, it didn't stop their corporate evil intent to put out our amazing bommy. As they roll out their long red/black hosepipes, shooting them off from all angles over our months'-long hard work, we, to the tune of 'Auld Lang Syne', chorally chant *Go home y'bums, go home y'bums, go home y'bums, go home.* Picking up anything we can grab, we angrily hurl it in their direction (looking back, seems it wasn't just the law we had a beef with: it was everyone who wasn't us!). Those mean arl-arse firemen leave a much-reduced bonfire, but even they aren't able to put it completely out. Our bommy is as indomitable as we are. So much so, next day it's still smouldering.

Whenever something as exciting as Bommy Night was happening I couldn't/wouldn't sleep. So, on November 6th, I'm the first one up and once again sneaking criminal-like from 6A to wander around what was left of last night's towering inferno (Blackstock Gardens cockily boasted the biggest of the tenement bommys, but then every tenement did). The sky's a purpling, mourning dark and noxious scents of burning coat everything, this damp stench a dank, misting companion. Meandering around the still spark-sputtering embers of our now feebling hell-storm, there's no one but me. Remembering the previous evening's dancing furies, I conjure a sense of historically-linked belonging... (Even as a kid, I lived for that sense of past life connection; my young head was never empty and the more emotively atmospheric a situation, the more I could spill my imagination all over it. As thought duvets go, such moments are the most wraparound beautiful.) The important thing for me is to be around what's left of our ailing, fading bommy. After all we'd done, been through, and even though those bothersome boys of fire brigade had tried their best to ruin it, a smidgeon of what we created is still with me. The bommy 'n' I aren't fully extinguished and I wholeheartedly cherish that.

Head round-shouldered bowed to the ground, I plod about our square looking for, picking up and smelling used fireworks. Rained-on wet, burst-open blackened and long-gone dead, I feel a bit sorry for their loss, so much so I actually talk to them. Consolingly whispering in what might pass for their just-blasted-off ears, I lovingly tell them how beautiful they'd so recently been.

'Gerrid killed the bommy!'

IX

'Gerrid lad, it's Jimmy...'

Early summer, June 5th 1970.

Few people are around, so must be off school. Nothing new there, I'm forever off school. I'm alone on our 'oller and relishing being alone on our 'oller; this rocky piece of barren waste ground always feeling kinda earthy ancestral. I'm rickety-rocking away on an old, broken pub chair, probably daydreaming about old, broken ancestors, when called over by, I think, Kitty Day. I say *think* because right now, for some strange reason, I can't quite picture her face. I know that sounds odd, but I genuinely can't. My gut feeling though is that it is Mrs Day. Kitty's a legendary Blackstock Gardens figure; rake thin, incredibly beautiful, cheekbones of a Grecian goddess, haloed by wonderfully dark, wavy hair. She's also mother of twelve wildly madcap kids, among them my mates Bernard 'n' Alec. The closer I get to her the more uncomfortable everything starts to feel. She's emotionally tense, the A-line of her skirt oddly angular; something's very wrong. She speaks; her voice is vulnerably careful and so softly authoritative I without question believe her: 'You've gorra get 'ome lad, straight 'ome now Gerrid. It's your Jimmy, something's 'appened.'

I don't ask what, can't, but in a flash know it's bad; worried women's eyes tell a whole story. I instantly know Kitty's internally/externally concerned, immediately know everything's completely different, instinctively know something terrible has happened to my brother and think I already know what.

I'm too nervously agitated to go straight to 6A and don't. I make my first port of call the Gregorys' flat to see our Janet, as Jimmy 'n' Janet recently moved from Kirkby back into Janet's Ma's. I'm thinking, *whatever's happened, if not Janet, then others will know; her sister Kathleen's bound to be there.*

Blackstock Gardens suddenly feels too tall, too wide; everything sharply skewwhiff and off-centre. What should take minutes seems to be taking hours. Simply getting to the Gregorys' is blurring a jaggedly-confusing forever. Surrounding walls are in my way and I'm bumping into them like an out-of-control dodgem. The many factories lined along Blackstock Street look red brick woeful, physically incorrect and, like Kitty's skirt, weirdly angled. Even the pavement feels wrong; softer, doughy and difficult to navigate. I get to the Gregorys' part of the tenement and slowly stride up the stairwell, its steps bending inwards like mushy rubber. People are crowded at their door. I immediately recognise a couple of Janet's brothers and although there's volume it all feels a muted, church-like silent. There's a bizarre disquiet coming from within the flat; different noises, muffled noises I've not heard before. Sadness burrows into sound: when grief invades it changes our voices, changes us, rounds our shoulders, bends our backs, contorts our faces. It's as if we instantly, naturally/unnaturally shift, becoming easier to read than traffic lights.

Then it explodes. Stopping me in my tracks, a forcefield blast of such mournful intensity pushing me away. I hear big crying, a woman's agonised sobs and the choral, arms-around scrum of consoling family. Although somewhat stunned, I realise this their private moment, their unique time 'n' place and immediately turn back.

Now I definitely know but don't have the words and, if did, don't think I can put them together or say them out loud. It's never *just* words; it's what they mean, how they hit; always, your stomach. The way it aggressively fills, like your body's full of knuckle-dusted, pug-ugly street-fighters. Whenever anything went wrong, my immediate response was to skedaddle straight back home. 6A always meant safety, sanctuary, but not this time. For some reason I want to be as far away from there as possible. Deliberately detouring, I walk through the massive arch from Blackstock Street leading to our other big square. I love this arch, always dark and comforting, my own private Batcave. For a short while I rest my back against its damp wall, but soon find that when thinking the worst there is no rest. Knowing there won't be anybody around, I need the wide-open width 'n' breadth of our other square.

I step from the dripping intimacy of my Batcave and the world immediately bright-light opens out. I'm suddenly in a wonderfully wide space, looking to the sumptuous blue of a fluffy-white-clouded sky and, for the briefest moment, solace. No matter my mood, the bold enormities of Blackstock Gardens always comfort and just the simple act of looking up eases. Looking up now though, I can see across the square through 6A's kitchen window and, within, a lot of shuffling, animated activity. From this distance it seems shadowy full, but certainly not upbeat, payday, party-shaped. Looking down with hyper-clarity, I clock the usual broken glass, splintered gravel, halfies (Scouse for 'half bricks') 'n' dog shit. There seems to be so much more of it and the broken glass looks murderous, as if lying in wait to slice me open. Kicking away glass, stones, halfies and dog shit was an everyday sport; we'd kick them at each other. This time though, kicking them from me feels like protection. The simplest of journeys becomes an impossible-to-negotiate assault course, everything uncertain, jagged, jutting and blocking. I eventually reach the familiar shade of our stairwell and, although being only four short flights to 6A, they've never looked steeper or more mountainous. Arching backwards, ready to pull myself upwards, I grab the railing. A repetitively retching sensation has me step-by-step gulping, my mouth watering and near-throwing up. Am I going to be sick, cry, laugh, completely break down, fidget, or should I make every-body a cup of tea? Right now, I don't know anything and it might be the very first time I've never known anything. Although only three flats long, it's a lengthy landing and 6A's the furthest apartment from the stairs. Outside, the blurry shapes of three men; my brothers' mates. They look baggy, misshapen, defeated. Two of them, chins sunken into their chests, lean sadly on the sill of our landing, whilst the other, smoking, his back against the wall, gazes downwards. The pathway to 6A feels longer, greyer than ever before, and a part of me hopes it never ends, but end it finally does and as per, our door's open. I look up and my brother's mates are ashen grey, their faces wrong. The one smoking, half-smile scuffs my hair and it's immediately comforting. 'Alright Gerrid,' he says. 'Y'better go in lad.'

I look to our doorway and I'm frightened. The noises coming from within immediately disturb me. Different to the noises at the Gregorys', brutally muddied, more masculine, hurried, confused and pained. 6A feels much taller/wider and a strange whining distortion builds inside/outside my head. If sound or vision can't be trusted then what can? It takes a very few steps to get from our tiny hallway to the kitchen and I don't want to take them. Whatever that noise, I don't wanna be part of it. But whatever that noise, I am part of it.

I immediately recognise everybody because I've always known them, they've always been there, but suddenly they're all someone else. They're still my mother, Big John, Thomas, Chris 'n' Paul, but they're clearly not, because my mother, Big John, Thomas, Chris 'n' Paul have never looked so incorrect. Kids are much cleverer than we think and although not knowing the word, what I clearly see is *despair*. More than see, I *sense* it, hanging heavy in near unbreathable air.

May is sat on her chair making the oddest noises. I try to focus, to hone in on and decipher what she's saying. She's manically repeating *no*, pneumatically mumbling it, sometimes over but always constantly under her breath. There's something unintelligible about her persistent babbling, her frightened murmurings making it sound like one long continual train crash of a word. In the middle of those physically scrunched-up utterances, she suddenly spills out, 'Not Jimmy, oh God, not my poor Jimmy.'

Normally, when walking into the room she's instantly overjoyed to see me. Not this time though. She's just sat, rocking back 'n' forth, her arms flailing an occasional, almost reckless, directionless. Our Chris is desperately trying to comfort her, but she keeps on shoving him off, pushing him away. All my brothers' faces are different, looking instantly older, emotionally shattered, and the big, mad, boisterous fuss usually made of me when skipping into our kitchen's not there. None of them hurl me up high, I'm neither thrown into another brother's arms nor acrobatically twisted onto their shoulders. They're not gonna do that this time. There are others, obviously friends and neighbours, but there's something so immediate-familial shared by my mother, brothers and I that whatever this is, it can only be about us. In amongst all the noisy, busying shapeliness, me 'n' my family are all the same shape.

Big John softly plonks me down on our couch but, like Kitty Day before him, I can't quite conjure his face; can see his perfect quiff mind, but not his funny old handsome face. Odd isn't it? I can clearly clock everybody else's visages; maybe the trauma of moment's blocking out the people who are gonna tell me what's actually happened. Big John gently takes me by my arms and, in a vocal tone full of protective feeling, says, 'Gerrid lad, it's Jimmy…'

I know what dead means. Being brought up a Vauxhall/Scottie Road Catholic saw to that. I was long used to seeing hearses leave from flats. Over our Blackstock Gardens landing you'd often see beginnings/endings; life/death an everyday ubiquitous spectacle with christenings/funerals liberally peppering the year. This feels like a different kind of dead though. An in-house dead, a far-too-near and too-much-a-part-of-me dead. This dead wasn't an elderly, sweets-giving neighbour, it's my brilliant, oldest brother. I'm completely blank after being told, totally unengaged, but immediately think, *I'll never again on the wall see our Jimmy's shadow, warming his arse against the fire.*

What was home becomes a busy tube station at rush hour, a kind of slow-motion rush hour where everything feels strangely becalmed yet manically hurried. There are lots of people passing, the gentle shove of hips, offers of a million boiled ham sandwiches, beer bottle tops flicking open and cigarettes repeatedly lit 'n' shared. Mouths quietly mumble chatter, looking like they're miming conversation. The smell of scouse is eternally simmering and, as if by magic, with his accordion, Uncle Chris is sat on the couch. He's not gonna play anything yet, now's not quite the time; he'll know exactly when. The noise around me, although madly reverberating, comforts, and I love and got lost in it. More than anything else, all these people care; I know I'm being genteelly talked to by somebody, lots of somebody's probably, but not taking anything in. I'm now too involved in the gathering collective energy to be interested in any one person. And it is energy, crackling 'n' alive, like a desperately sad Bommy Night.

May is completely lost, her eyes looking beyond walls to other places. Because so many people are around, I can't get to her and maybe don't want to. I'm still trying to work out what's going on. So much big information is coming thick 'n' fast.

Our Jimmy is definitely dead. He died falling from his place of work on the demolition. Our Chris has been at the hospital and is constantly being asked questions, and the poor fella's doing his shocked best to answer. I clearly see he doesn't want to. Everybody seems enormously tall and in some sort of control. This is a community historically/presently knowing death, how it works, what to do when it kicks off, and I'm slowly starting to get that. Suddenly want to cry but can't, everything is too out in the open and this is way too personal. Anyway, no one wants to see a stupid kid whinging. I know I'm in the right place because there is no other place, but don't quite know what to do. Because somebody's told a joke there's explosive bursts of laughter; feels odd, sounds ugly, not in keeping with the situation, but maybe there's gotta to be jokes. Like all Scousers, our Jimmy loved jokes, told jokes; perhaps they're just fondly repeating his favourites, so maybe I'm wrong. I start to feel wrong and am slowly disappearing. I continually overhear *he was too young, a brilliant footballer*, like it's on some kind of mournful repeat. Although a brilliant footballer, our Jimmy wasn't young. They've got that wrong and it's making me angry. He's really old. Twenty-nine.

Some women are openly crying and some men look like they have been. It's a new world, but one I'm instantly involved and uninvolved in. Sounds to me women's voices know more than men's. They know what to exactly say and where to put whatever it is wherever it has to be put and, more importantly, how 'n' why you have to put it there. Mary Mac is great with everything 'n' everyone; what me Ma can't do she's doing for her. She's making people feel right at home. Mary possesses so much natural authoritative wit and I'm more than made up she's around. She using her laugh to comfort people and is expert at it. Repetitive waves of sadness ripple, a mixture of silence and noise which, when colliding, completely fills our tiny kitchen. Everything is as beautiful as ugly. People continue knocking on our door, bringing things on plates. There's not much room, but miraculously they get in. In/around wide, wet eyes there is so much bloodshot sadness and knowing. Inside me, my ribs start trembling, my spine buckles and I begin to panic.

*

Pretty sure she's the Collins's, but could've been the Malones'. Pretty sure her name's Queenie, but may well be Sheba. Whoever's she is, whatever her name, this dog loves me and I her (because I'm gay I'll to refer to her as Queenie).

In the sixties, dogs, like kids, were left to run feral-free. You would often see them collect wild in packs, running each other down, madly barking for dominating, neck-biting position. Queenie, an incredibly handsome Alsatian, is old and wise. This long-in-the-fang bitch soft-padded her own path, a path often leading to me. So often in fact, people passing would ask if she's my dog and sometimes I cheekily say *yes*.

I've had to get out of 6A. I'm sat at the bottom of the tenement with my head buried in the damp, musky whiff of Queenie's fur. My energy's different tonight and she knows I'm sad. Sat, she's taller than me, her ears a sharply-twisting alert, her long, lolloping-tongue keeping a more comforting yet drooling sense of time. Blackstock Gardens is generously doing what it always does. Such the wide-open expanse of its construction it once again has its arms around me. That long beleaguered, much scorched corporation light, high-hanging in the middle of the square, ambers a round, soft glow. It looks a lot like how we were taught souls might appear and I wonder if it's our Jimmy's.

Not sure I know what this kind of sadness is, but it's everywhere; feel it in the cold, damp ground we're sitting on. It's June, dry and warm, have my tears made it wet? I'm uneasily hyper-vigilant and can see every red brick in every wall and the crumbling, surrounding cement. Don't know what never seeing our Jimmy ever again in all actuality means. Where's he gone, heaven? I'm constantly told about heaven, I believe in heaven. At school we crayon pictures of it, therefore I should know all about it, at least where it is, but right now, I don't. People keep telling me that's where he is, sat with the angels and God. Although I wholeheartedly believe in angels and God, it's not sinking in. I just want to be arms-around next to him sat on his knee, want to hear his laughing voice; we laughed a lot. He'd bury his big, curly-haired head into my forehead, gently tickle me and we'd giggle. It was all too much in 6A, getting far too loud and grown-up. What's happening is a big grown-up thing and whilst I know I'm not being pushed away, I simply don't understand a lot of what's being said. So much of their complex, high-speed conversation is beyond me. I'm not an ignored kid, but in 6A I felt I wasn't needed. I'm sad too, dead sad, but can't do the same sad as them. I don't have the lengthy stories of growing up, don't know the jokes, don't know how to tell them, can't smoke the ciggies or drink the ale, I don't know the other words to those much older songs being so passionately sung. All I know was that I wanted to sing along.

It's excellent sitting on the pavement with Queenie. She's just solidly there, big breathing, protecting, looking out for and leaning into my forehead like our Jimmy would have. She's doing what I want my mother to do and I'm wondering if May will ever be able to do it again.

More than anything though, I just want my brother back.

X
Ninny Prescott

I'm cross-legged sat in an ornately wall-painted cave mouth. Flecked by the central colour of coal fire, all is a mythically dark, half-lit, cavernous still. The air's muddy with musky smells of incense, biting sniff of snuff and the perpetually bubbling swamps of ribs 'n' cabbage.

Placed into chiselled-out alcoves, underlit by red-'n'-blue-glassed candlelight, their softly painted faces enigmatically half-smiling, carefully angled statues stare down. Looking at me like she genuinely loves me, Our Lady's berry-pink lips, aquamarine eyes and ruddily rouged cheeks are especially affecting. There's something about the perfect mothering of the Blessed Virgin that kids without perfect mothers can immediately and with great intimacy latch onto. Appearing every inch the legendary listener he's famed to be, St. Gerard the Patron Saint of Good Confessions is quietly corner-stood. Although darker robed and an obviously hair-receding male, like Mary, Gerard is no less soft-smirking, hands held-high, holy. He's looking at me like he's already listened and I somehow think he has… well, I am named after him. Gerrids of an angel feather stick together.

Dominating one cave wall, a huge, black-lacquered, patent-leather-looking frame; within it a lush, pictorial vision of The Last Supper. Witnessing the Holy Spirit's sudden appearance, gasping, pointing, astonished-faced apostles have spooky flames flickering above their heads. Sitting centre stage, plagued by the horrors of his Biblically-foretold near future, a wisely resigned Jesus pontificates; sharing, telling and smugly accusing (watch out Thomas 'n' Judas!). Because of its obvious operatic melodrama, I immediately fall in love with this painting, imagining myself in it. With all those apostles appearing to me as brothers it looks like I've recently just lived it. Hung happily next door to this soon-to-be-doomed Jesus, there's another be-haloed and wounded-palmed, just-resurrected one. This newly reborn Jesus's frame is auburn-oaken, smoothly rounded; a tawny, oval cameo brooch, seeming a little more aesthetically effete than his big, butch, black-leather-clad neighbour. He's the eternal hope of these two pieces, there for an upbeat fairytale-ending reason; a sacred-hearted reminder to us all of Life Everlasting. As introductions to working class high art they are narratively brilliant retellings because, like most Catholic prints, they didactically insist on giving you an exact story.

Then it hits me. Statues, paintings, postcards, key rings or opaque Our Lady holy water bottles with big blue crowns… it doesn't matter. I am completely surrounded by the same slightly lopsided half-smile. Whatever the size, gender or sacred desig-nation, whether a Lourdes-bought ciggie-lighter or ashtray, even when facing the excruciating horror of certain crucifixion, every baring-down face has the same benignly knowing, ever so slightly smirking gob.

For some time now there's been a mind-boggling sense of being scooped up by a big godlike hand, quickly taken from one place and just as quickly plonked down into another. From the nicotine-stained walls of 6A, I've been suddenly teleported to a labyrinthine maze where pungent hits of hot-pot-simmering mystery haunt everywhere. Everything feels an ancient underneath, a forever below; I'm buried beneath huge religious boulders and the waters pouring down them, holy. You'd never in a million years think this Vatican crypt facsimile is an immaculately kept, ground-floor, two-bedroom council flat that my beyond houseproud Nin would hate me imagining a cave.

Ninny Prescott wore her soul on her home, and her sacrosanct objet d'art ephemera decoratively splatter everywhere. Her ornamental cabinet houses the most beautiful silver Holy Communion set I've ever born witness to. I stare in daily raptured, captured awe at just how intricately detailed this centrepiece crucifix appears. Looking a lot like a crisscrossing gleaming metal soul, it celestially shines, bringing you in until you become part of that shine. So obviously expensive, and clearly forged by His Holiness The Pope himself, my guess is it'd been lifted 'n' nicked straight from the Basilica.

From the hallway I peer around a door into Ninny Prescott's bedroom. She's sat on the edge of her bed with my mother kneeling in front of her. May appears young and broken, emotionally exhausted, her head upon her mother's thighs, looking to me like she'd done something unforgivably naughty and was clearly to blame. I'm no stranger to May being childlike, but I've never seen her shaped like one; no words are being exchanged and everything feels like heady prayer. Perhaps it's all the domineering Catholic imagery, but they look exactly like a scene from our favourite film, *The Song of Bernadette*. My middle-aged Ma seeming like a lost teenage handmaiden, innocently knelt at the foot of an all-knowing Madonna. As much as I want to, I know not to enter their sacred sanctum. This quiet communion they're clearly handsheld sharing is not about or for me. For the first time in days, my mother is exactly where she should be. Although a heartbroken shattered, she desperately needs her mam.

It's difficult to sequentially piece together. After the death of her first-born son May was continually falling to pieces. I remember in 6A, her arms outstretched, wailing at our kitchen wall, as I held onto her waist for dear life, thinking *if I let go she'll throw herself through the window*.

Concern for her was everywhere and we all thought the best thing to do was to get her to her mother's. Ninny Prescott lived only a twenty-minute walk down the road and so it would be easy to keep May abreast of anything going on at home.

I was told that I had to go with her and it instantly broke my heart. I seriously didn't want to, not because I didn't wanna protect me Ma, of course I did, but the thought of leaving Blackstock Gardens was crushing. I desperately wanted to stand alongside my brothers; not being around them before our Jimmy's funeral was anathema to me. I kicked up a whinging, hot-tempered fuss to stay. But go I had to; youngest son duty...

It takes four people to haul an increasingly fragile May to the waiting taxi. She's so physically rickety I honestly think she's going to break. Up till this point, I've never seen anyone so frightened; I'll never forget the gnarling mix of grief and agoraphobia squalled into her twisted face, looking like she'd been painted by Edvard Munch. After a lot of tortured emoting and May seeming like she's genuinely going to any-second snap, Big John and I finally get her into the cab. Once inside, her hand wraps so tightly around my wrist it hurts and she starts re-jibbering that same pained, elongated mumble. A concerned taxi driver stops and asks if she's okay. Big John quickly tells him what's happened and our cabby immediately understands. I'm beginning to read and recognise the communicative shorthand between adults a bit more. It seems most of the time they don't need a lot of words, just brief explanation; a scrunched-up face, then a kind-eyed, knowing nod.

Although completely attentive of May and more than aware of my fixed orders, there's a part of me really enjoying the grown-up thrill of my first taxi ride. I'm completely transfixed by the taxicab's meter ticking down, its clicking numbers an absurd sci-fi clock waiting to go boom. For the first time in what's seemed an agonising forever there's a travelling sense of adventure.

Lapworth Street's odd, much squatter in appearance than where we're from. It's only three-high apartment blocks, nowhere near as visually impressive as ours, with each looking like they need a good kick up the arse. I'm used to the Grand-Guignol-gothic-majesty of our stone-reddened, imposing tenement. Here seems flatter, greyer, quieter, giving off a more subdued, Sunday-afternoon feeling than a raucous, partying, weekend vibe. We're gonna be at Ninny Prescott's for a week, enough time for our Jimmy's funeral to have happened and be over. Although at first not wanting to go, it soon proves itself the right place to be.

I had always felt incredibly Catholic, relished Bible stories and completely believed in and loved Jesus. By now I'd been to confession, made my first Holy Communion and felt fully embraced by everything my religion could throw at me, but it was my Nin who'd make me even more religiously structured.

Ninny Prescott was a small, slight, be-pinnied woman, deaf as a post and spoke with the tiny voice of a startled bird, but possessed such visibly stoic authority you immediately knew not to cross her. I could clearly see everyone around trusted her and to this day I've not met a person who carried such naturally generous control. Nin hadn't always been Catholic, she was (God forgive her) a Protestant convert. I remember Nin smugly telling me *converts always made for better Catholics* and I readily believed her. But then she could have said Protestants made better tutu-wearing werewolves and I'd still have readily believed her. From a child's point of view that amount of faith held in one tiny body felt powerfully magical. Without ever having to say the word *Christ*, Ninny Prescott made me believe in him more than school/church ever did – and school/church had done a damn fine, leather-belt-strapping, cane-whupping job. Whatever faith was, it held every atom of my grandmother together; she was defined by it.

*

Sitting with my grandmother by the open fire in her darkened kitchen means the world. Huddle-crouched in a fireside-glowing, it feels like we're a Ladybird book illustration. Because an exhausted May is forever lying down, Nin and I spend a lot of bonding, quality time together. That is, until either my aunty or uncle enter the room.

Living with my grandma are my mother's sister 'n' brother, Aunty Esther and Uncle Chris. As much as my Nin is wonderful, these two by contrast are a complexly different story. Both internally troubled, these siblings don't really get on; more than anything they seem to reluctantly tolerate each other, and when we're all sat together everything suddenly feels uncomfortably strained.

Aunty Esther had some time ago lost a young child, Bernadette, to a tragic road accident and Uncle Chris, who had never got over being refused a place studying English at Cambridge University due to his pronounced stutter, was now recently estranged from his marital family. They're painfully difficult for me; Aunty Esther completely ignores me and, in my presence, Uncle Chris seems an edgy, uneasy-wary. I think I'm too girly for him. When pissed though, he's very different; a money-giving, non-stuttering, joke-telling, masterful accordion-playing joy. When rotten drunk, he seems to genuinely like me. Aunty Esther, on the other hand, just doesn't acknowledge my existence and at this particularly difficult time, it's hard to digest. I'm used to adults being incredibly kind to me, giving me untold amounts of sweets and not treating me like I'm invisible.

When they're in the same room as us, I watch in silent awe at what I think the strange Catholic witchcraft of my Nin is magically doing to them. My grandma, head slightly bowed, eyes up, just stares in their direction and, right in front, of me they slowly fall into an almost meditative, half-asleep quiet. Although their stories differ, the cold, stony intensities surrounding them are picturesquely similar: they both have no teeth and are sitting like the same hypnotised, cold, gummy statue. I'm now sure I can feel, almost *see*, an energy emitting from my Nin to her children, and it is this mystical Nin energy calming them down. After a couple of days of witnessing this and staring in wide-eyed wonder at my grandma, she eventually turns to me and says, 'You know, don't you?'

Now, I'm not sure what I'm supposed, without explanation, to actually *know*. I could literally *know* anything. I *know* my aunty/uncle are historically/presently emotionally distressed. I *know* to be silent to accommodate said distress. But, if she meant it was her magically/mystically controlling the depressed moods of her unhappy children, then yes, I do *know* that too. When spying on her from the hallway into the bedroom, it's the same thing she's doing to May. Before arriving at me Nin's, clearly upset and grieving, me Ma was a flat-out, broken mess. But, like a tossed-about junk might after a storm, in her mother's healing presence she suddenly becalms.

My favourite of Nin's stories also concerned another of my mother's deceased sons, our Vincent. At four years of age, after falling down a very few steps, Vincent Butler died from his resulting head/brain injuries. May was uncontrollably distraught and immediately sought the alleviating solace of her mother. Nin told me that for days there was no consoling her devastated daughter, 'Gerard, I'd never seen anyone like it in me life, she was in an awful state, but I'll never forget the night she finally found peace.'

After one of many sobbing nights, May was lying down when suddenly, and as if someone had gently sat on it, she felt the end of her bed slightly sag. Looking up and ahead in what seemed a dim, golden light, me Ma saw, seated with his back to her, the shoulders and head of a toddler. Recognising this spectral kid's dirty blond curls, she immediately knew that it was Vincent.

Nin told me, 'And no word of a lie Gerard, let God strike me down dead, from then onwards your mother stopped grieving, didn't cry another drop. She came to me the next day, telling me what'd happened and I straight away told her. I said, *that was little Vincent that May, who's now an angel in heaven, telling us he's alright and to stop your fretting*.' My mother would back up this story many times and every time she told it I'd believe her a little bit more. Whatever its familial legitimacy, and I now think it was a necessary hallucination, it doesn't stop the level of miraculously embossed storytelling I was brought up on. On top of what I'd witnessed from her with Aunty Esther and Uncle Chris, yet another mysteriously gothic ghost story told by my wise auld Nin made her seem the most magical woman alive. God, I adored her; always two steps ahead aware, a cunning woman indeed.

One fireside night she told me, 'You do know, don't you Gerard, you're a seventh son, your mother's a seventh child, you were born in July, the seventh month, and G for Gerard's the seventh letter of the alphabet?' I replied, 'No Nin, I don't.' She said, 'Well lad, I think it best you should!' Couldn't stop herself, could she? Now seven steps ahead, she was doing her witchy, healing schtick on me.

Surrounded by hugely ornate pictorial Catholicism and a heavenly choir of holy statues, flanked by big, white, lit candles, I watch in complete astonishment as, in her living room, my now knelt Nin takes Holy Communion off an actual priest. Then, seeing big, burly Father Flynn using the Communion set from the cabinet, holding its silver salve under her chin, blows my tiny mind. I think it the most powerful, human-shaped image I've ever witnessed. In my Catholic schoolboy head; priests are at the very top of the local community ladder, they've all the God-like power possible. They certainly don't come to your Nin's house to perform Mass. I'm not an easily upset or scared child but, like most kids, incredibly wary of our parish priests. Perhaps priests in Lapworth Street are nicer than anywhere else or, better still, has my good witch of a Nin put a spell on him too?

They're both bathed in an incandescently divine aura and I'm bowled over by the intense religiosity of it all. This is what witnessing a bona fide miracle must feel like. The air is thick as treacle and everything about them an all-encompassing holy. Breaking through this angelically chorused vision comes an operatic, bass baritone, as a deep Dublin brogue says *Body of Christ* and my Nin sing-song tweets back *Amen*.

After this other-worldly, near-heavenly ceremony, the priest takes a bottle of Guinness then sits with Nin. Compared to a towering, broad-shouldered, silver-haired Father Flynn, Nin seems even tinier, but she still solidly leads the conversation. Father Flynn sups 'n' nods along and not in a patronising way. It seems to me he's genuinely relishing her council. On the couch opposite, big-beam smiling and looking like she's witnessed the exact same miraculous moment, sits Aunty Esther. When it's all over and she starts to leave, I excitedly stand up to say something about it and, as if I'm not in the room, she simply walks past me.

Like she has been all week, me Ma is still lying on grandma's bed, but we are going back home to Blackie in the morning. To May's favourite-son-delight, Big John has visited to tell us about Jimmy's funeral. I know that he's been buried (the word *buried* sounding so brutal), but because of being at Nin's I can imagine he hasn't. Here I can everyday daydream he's still alive; going back is gonna make him being dead all too real again.

It's Sunday eve and in the kitchen it's just me, my Nin, a raging coal fire, and what's left of the flickering remains of a minor miracle. Ninny Prescott, not for the first time, gives me the tiniest drop of her Guinness, takes a sniff of snuff off o' the back of her hand, and quietly sits with me. It's unusual her sitting still because she's forever in the back-kitchen cooking; endless pans of scouse of course, but her rabbit 'n' barley soup and pea 'n' ham shank broth are to die for. You don't even have to eat them, just their thick stench steaming up the room fills your stomach. I adore being in her back-kitchen, it's a safe space, and daily mesmerised by her on-the-wall, push-button tealeaves dispenser; just one press and a fast rush of tea falls into her teapot. I think it far too modern a device for someone as antiquated as her.

Sat on her chair and seemingly from nowhere, Nin breaks my abstraction: 'Your mother's going to need a lot of looking after and it's going to be mostly you doing it, y'know that don't you Gerard? It won't always be easy on you lad, but she's your mother and worth it.' I don't think me Nin knows quite how much of that I've been doing but, with my eyes peering from above my mug and gingerly supping my delicious Guinness, I nod in knowing agreement.

Although never wanting to leave 6A in the first place, now I'm not so sure I want to go back. My grandma's shown me a brand new world of Christ and how the inbuilt resurrections of Christian magics can make the impossible happen. Who knows, like Jesus, perhaps my brother's come back from the dead. I've become fairytale-embedded in Nin's underground, soup-aroma'd catacombs, in her birdsong enchantments and spell-casting. It has allowed me to occasionally forget.

XI
There's No Place Like...

Any sense of meaningful rest is completely off the cards. Night after night holding on to a heaving, sobbing mother means until the heaving, sobbing stops I can't even think of sleep and mostly don't.

It's probably six-thirty in the morning, May's building the fire and outside our front door 'Ob-la-di, Ob-la-da' is being whistled by our young milk boy, Colin Blundell. Like every kid, Colin's well known in Blackie, with me Ma often calling him a little Mickey Rooney: 'Should be on the telly, that lad.' Colin certainly possesses Rooney's innate sense of musicality. Pitch-perfectly ricocheting around the natural reverb of our landings and, mixed-in with the surprisingly in-time, chiming clink of milk bottles (he's proper showin' off), Colin's rendition of this popular Beatles melody is a most uplifting, welcoming sound.

Maybe I've gotten too used to the huddled, bubbling, cauldron-like Catholicism of my Nin's flat, but right now 6A feels different. Everything's empty, far too bright and everywhere unreachably tall. At seven years old, you can't intellectually know it's not the rudimentary dimensions of your home that's changed but the people in it; every one of us experiencing cathedral-sized feelings in a rickety arl garden shed too small to house them. There's an escalating dream/nightmare sense of size and time distorting. I'm constantly looking at my mother to guide her to a chair before, on strange angles, she falls to wherever the floor may have been and once again starts wailing.

Our Chris and Paul wake up for work and they're chaotically shuffling, puffy-eyed, half-blinded and lifeless; it might be they're hungover, but it's not like them at all. I'm still not going to school and won't for another year, but before Jimmy died and after their tea 'n' toast, I'd normally be hurled about everywhere, perhaps even hung over our landing by an arm and leg. Don't get me wrong, them hanging me over our landing by my arm and leg terrified the living daylights outta me, but I'd give an arm and leg for them to be doing that very thing right now. Any amount of screeching, childlike fear is far preferable to this grieving, zombie-ing nowhere.

Although our Thomas is still living with us, he's now spending a lot more time at his fiancée Angela's. I'm seriously missing him and his bossy, early morning, dad-like ways. If anyone could get Chris 'n' Paul to hang me over our landing it was deffo him: 'Right you two, get our Gerrid over that fuckin' landin' now... d'ye 'ear me? NOW!'

When other people are around, May is able to pull herself together a little bit; it's when they leave she fully crumbles. With Chris and Paul out the door and off to work she almost stumbles backwards into her chair. She round-shoulders shrinks, one arm tightens around her waist while the other lifts to her face. Putting thumb to mouth, she once again starts mumbling. Droning on 'n' on, repetitively rocking, she looks to window's daylight and is gone. It feels like I'm forever watching her disappear and, although preferable to some of the heightened emotional states she can get in, her daily vanishings fill me with emptying gloom. It used to be a different story, not anything like this.

Before our Jimmy's death, when being kept off school, I'd sit behind May playing with her pinny-strings and watching the telly. There was a wealth of early morning school programmes and at dinnertime the BBC's wondrous 'Watch wi' Ma': *Andy Pandy, Trumpton, The Herbs, The Woodentops, Paulus the Wood-gnome* and *Pogles' Wood*, to name a non-stop, stop-frame animated, string-puppeting few. May was great at all this magical kids' telly and forever improvising games from what we were viewing. I'd even love it when the telly *goes out* and needs money. May would tightly wrap a silver shilling in my hand to put in the meter and it'd feel like being adult. I really got off on the always-difficult-to-twist, wide, metal dial of the meter and thrilled to hear the soft, tinny thud of my coin landing on all those other long-dormant silver shillings; felt like my silver shilling was joining its long-lost gang. Hanging on for a bit behind the telly, through a dusty brown hardboard, hole-dotted grill and as if getting ready to secretly party, I'd watch its valves slowly relighting. There was always a faint smell of static when those valves came back on, a slightly woody, sulphuric scent I thought mystical.

We'd often watch school programmes aimed at much older children and both be goggle-eyed glued. May loved being a talkative narrator so, when seeing a baby being blood-howling born, she'd tell me in minute 'n' experiential detail that this was how it exactly was for women and that childbirth had nothing to do with being found under a cabbage or being brought to you by some stupid bastard'n stork: 'Rubbish all tha' Gerrid, absolute rubbish, sometimes we even shit ourselves!'

When music shows came on she'd immediately start dancing, getting me up with her; we'd joyfully boogie away to skiffle, jazz, Cilla, or maybe even Polish folk tunes. After a bout of fun-filled jigging, she'd arms-outstretched 'n' twirling tell me that when she was a kid she had wanted to run away with a troupe of gypsy performers to dance in deserts around the world. Being from Liverpool and so near the docks, around the world felt next door to us, especially to me Ma's generation. They/we were forever being regaled by drunken ex-merchant seamen with their tall-ship tales of exotic locale.

There wasn't anything exotic about her right now though. She looked like a lumpy, five-pound bag of moulding King Edwards.

'Gerrid, it's the nuns!'

Their knock recognisable as my name and, although slightly fearful of the charity-collecting abbesses, they're always able to shock May from the capture of her chair. She likes they're Irish and has always been onto their conniving politeness. Even though nervous of them, they somehow same-time 'n' same-knock weekly reassure her.

It takes a bit of clumsy-fumbling doing but, with me by her side, we get to and open the door. It's always a peculiar moment greeting the sisters; I'm as small any seven-year-old can be and every adult's bigger than me except, it seems, these three smirking nuns. I'm not saying they aren't taller, they must be, but huddled together like they are they certainly don't tower. The sisters have heard about our Jimmy and whatever their holy/financial motivations, their condolences and assurance that he's now sat with Our Lord in heaven mean the world to May. The nuns speak in thin-voiced, tuneful unison, a bit like Irish Beverley Sisters in wimples. Even trilling *Goodbye May, God bless now* seems a gently head-nodded choral and liltingly half-sung in winsome, tinny-voiced harmony.

We've a little bit of money coming into the house now, so May delights in passing it on. This visit, one of the nuns has given her a relic medal of St. Anthony, apparently housing a tiny piece of fabric once touching his entombed bones. For as long as I can remember, May would keep their precious medal in the loving cave of her purse. That battered, red/brown, big white-stitched, leather purse, made for her in school by one of Annie King's sons, is May's sacred place; her soul in physical form. Believe me, if anything other than money got in there it was incredibly special.

These days and nights are liberally peppered by visitors looking in on my mother. Cousin Ellen, Uncle Chris's daughter, is just lovely. A beautiful young woman with fantastically dark wavy hair, forever wearing the most genuine smile and always full of gifts. She's as fond of my mother as May is of her. She's fantastic with me too, bringing me silver 'n' gold wrapped sweets 'n' toffees – and not the sweets 'n' toffees I'm normally used to. Because they're shiny I think they're a bit posh. Always in her hand, tied together by a thin blue ribbon, is a Sayers box of fresh cream cakes. Whenever given a cake, I instinctively know to sit behind the table on the wooden step under our kitchen window. I'm getting really good at knowing when adults need their space and, biting into an ingredients-spurting custard slice, I watch Ellen and May jangle. They talk to each other so heads-leaning-in quietly, so passionately intently, their words sound like another language; one only they spoke. With some people May can get slightly more confessional about things and our Ellen's certainly one of them. I could well be wrong here, but Ellen may have once considered becoming a nun. Though that might be because we've just said goodbye to them.

Aunty Esther often calls and, whilst completely blanking me, is great company for my mother. Having also lost a young child, the intense psychic communication, unspoken and around that, between these two sisters/mothers is just theirs; only they know what loss like that can possibly mean. May definitely has that *other* connection with her eccentric sibling.

From my ledge I watch as Aunty Esther's hand slowly reaches into her bag and, within its battered, brown leather, I hear the unmistakable rustle of sweets unwrapping. Then, like she thinks no one can see, but everyone clearly can, she sneakily puts the now naked boiled sweetie into her mouth. It's one of many quirks she has and I can't understand why she won't offer me or anybody else one. But like everything with family, no matter how eccentric their behaviour, you're born to get used to it. However she is with me right now simply doesn't matter; she's welcome, comforting respite for my mother and therefore for me, so useful after all.

Neighbours pop in almost hourly, often with gifts and no end of food stuffs. Everyday, wrapped in tea towels, plates of something with another plate over it are given over to my mother. Sometimes there's sprinklings of conversation, bursts of laughter, but more often than not an intense companionable silence... plenty of mothers around our way had lost kids.

Today is Washing Day, when most of the Blackstock Gardens women clean the outside of their flats' winders (Scouse for 'windows'). Even though our tenement's a tall, five-stories high, from ground to fifth, they somehow lean/hang by their knees right out of their winders. With their backs to the ground and no fear of height, tattered arl chamois leather in hand, they happily pink-Windolene away. It's an incredibly dangerous thing to be weekly doing; health 'n' safety gone invisible. These council flat windows are framed a thin metal rickety and a lot of these women hanging out of them are big women, but every week *do their winders* they diligently do. There's a mixture of ages from very young to very old and most of them are kind of communicating. They're not quite chatting; it isn't their normal street corner, sweet shop jangle, just lots of nods, shouts, shrieks, and howls of echoing laughter (a bit like our Rush noises). Some whistle or sing and, because of the circling, physical similarities winders-washing entails, there's an expansive sense of musical film choreography about it all. To this camp kid, sat on our wooden step and peering out our winder, our other square now looks like a scene from an epic Hollywood musical. Lionel Bart could have written what I'm witnessing. Once again, women being completely fascinating, not just for being mothers or wives, but because they possess/ represent such courageous, up-tempo spectacle.

When first starting Our Lady's Infants, after being taken for the first time by Mary Mac, I'd then have to make my own way up a dauntingly long Vauxhall Road. It was a good ten/fifteen minutes' walk from Blackstock Gardens to school, but every day the women of Tate & Lyle sugar refiners would be marching along that road to their shifts. It couldn't have been but it felt like there were hundreds of them (millions in my head), who when seeing me, duffle-coat hooded, scuffed-shoe shuffling alone to school, would scoop me up, asking if I was alright. They were immediately hands-held concerned for my safety and forever giving me sweets. I'd march shoulder-to-hip with them and some would stop at the top of Eldon Street, where they'd watch me infant-mince up it to school. The infectious chattering laughter of them is a noise I still imaginatively hear, often a noise I need to hear.

Always loved looking out of our window on Washing Day, but after what's recently happened, I love it even more. They immediately cheer me up; those all-singing, all-chattering, all-winders-cleaning, heavy-duty matriarchs making me beam from ear to ear, their real-life musical making me confidently camper. God, they're fabulous!

Our Janet and Kathleen, her inseparable sister and irrepressible bezzie, would always weekly visit. If you could apply the word *carnival* to anybody it would be to Kathleen Gregory. One of the funniest people I've ever known and, in a city of so many seasoned vaudevillian broads, that's an accolade indeed. Mary Mac somehow psychically knew when they'd be popping round and would always either be there just before or turn up soon after they arrived. All three were superbly skilled, Scottie/Vauxhall Road, sit-down comics, and the combination of them together on our couch was a belly-laugh massacre. Kathleen and Mary especially seemed not only to know everything about everybody's business but knew why knowing what they knew was outrageously the most hysterical thing ever. Funny storytelling is a centuries-passed-down

Scouse thing and these two, still-young-veterans, high mistresses of the craft. When it was just me, me Ma, Janet, Kathleen, Mary Mac and little baby Cathy, it was all completely raucous. So much so, May would often be screeching/hissing out, 'Oh, c'mon now girls, stop it, stop it now will'yz; you've got me pissin' me meself 'ere!' Their freeing animation filled the room. There were even tag-team-like grabbing-each-other moments, followed by wickedly spot-on punchlines with riotously roaring heads thrown back 'n' howling. The infectiously brassy tonic of that laughter always so happily healing. There was no booze, just endless cups of tea supplied by me, so when this lot got together it was more of a fun-filled party than any alcohol-fuelled do. And what rollickingly ripe, no-holds-barred language they used! I can still hear the power of it. So confidently rude and speedily delivered, this was high octane swearing as fire-crackling, howl-abounding poetry.

Not today though, not right now.

Their first visit after being at Nin's isn't anything like a spot-lit vaudevillian stage. It feels heavy-draped and curtains down, a theatre gone dark. Janet has just lost her husband, my mother her son and, although two very different relationships, the looks on their faces, especially when greeting each other, is equally heartbreaking. What kids see in pictures makes up for language they don't have and I clearly see a weave of bleakness covering everybody. There's such a cold dank weight to it, making everywhere feel suddenly rained-on wet. I'm still making the tea, my job, but instead of madly ricocheting laughter, it's all stuttering mumbles and sobbing. There's still a lot of reaching out mind, not to carry on the joke or pass over a punchline, but to hold and comfort. A lot of the conversation's about the funeral, the church service and how well it had gone, about how hot it was and our Jimmy's body discolouring. Although I didn't know what that meant, hearing it punches me in the stomach. The grief of them repeatedly monsoons our kitchen and, not possessing the words or memories they have, means I can't help but once again feel distanced; I'm sat, unmoving, with an unearthly sense of being pulled away from them. Kathleen and Mary still throw in the odd funny line – someone always does something ridiculous or gets too pissed at a Scouse wake. Strangest thing though, through all of this, I can clearly see a thick, black light connecting May and Janet together. Janet's a young, beautiful woman, still radiant even in black-clad mourning clobber, and me Ma, slightly hunched and beginning to crone. But right now, bathed by this darkest of lights, they are the same age, the same person. I wished me Nin was here, she'd deffo see it too. Not only that, I'm sure she would have been magically able to turn that black light off.

I must have still been playing out with my nephews and friends but I can't recall any of that. Being surrounded by all this adult sadness took up most of my time. I was always going to look after me Ma, but now I'd promised Nin there could be no reneging on that deal. Anyway, the whole wide world was happening all at once in 6A, so while I might have been out playing with friends it would have been as nothing to what was continually unravelling at home. My other brothers were increasingly different; no strangers to booze, but they were drunk a lot more now, and a once-volatile May, a cardigan-mound of sorrowful sobbing.

6A was still filling with people; it's what happens when someone dies, especially a young someone, and I can't put into words how much I loved the noise of that. Everything is/was different though. I'm not saying I felt grown up, in many ways I'd never felt more a child but, along with that brutally evolving *everything*, I was also changing.

I would, whenever I could, sneak out a little more often. The silence in 6A could frequently bully and pummel, the choking stillness of it exhausting. I was used to a partying house full of confident Scouse sound and animated familial reverie, not this long-tunnelled mausoleum of mourning. Sneaking outside to my beloved Blackstock Gardens and, by proxy, even further afield to my soon-to-be-beloved Dock Road gave me back some of those familial experiences. Just physically being around buoyant Scousers going to the pub, on their way to the match, on a message or talking on corners, started to feel more 'n' more like escape. Often when the flat filled and it got too language-ing adult, I'd fly (Scouse for 'go') to the Dock Road. Mainly because I loved how shadowy-tall everywhere gargantuan was, how much Mersey and magnificent sky I could see. And let me tell you somethin' f'nottin', dockland skies never sky the same sky twice. Here, people just did ordinary things. They may have been hiding it, but they didn't look full of face-aching, belly-wretched emotion. I flew to and around the Dock Road a lot.

XII
Paul's Fall

Inside of her body is on the outside of her body and I'm flung from sob to howl to yell. Inhale breath fast; gasp it in quick because I don't know when I next can. Noise is blocked out, then clear-eared, and once again flooded by weighty drench of cardigan. I'm crushed, scrunched, inescapably knotted in this violent Gordian body and having to take the blows. I'm a possum in a maelstrom, a rattling dice banging about in tumbler made from mother. Pushed, pummelled, pulped and having to stay stillest I've ever been. Can't scream, mustn't; this ragged jostling isn't about me, I promised my Nin. It's in her back, belly and breast. The grinding sound of loss unending, unforgiving.

I'm on first name terms with this subterranean inhumanity. Can hear Jimmy, can hear Vincent, can hear Joan. Everyday told the stories, grown covered in their repetitively resonating tortures. Lived them, loved them, know where they seed, root, blossom 'n' boom. Every sob a punch, every breath a death, every deity cursing howl a desperately begging plea: 'God no, please God no, how can you do this to me, not again, not again, please no, take me this time, if y'have to take anybody, take me!' Her arms clench my back. Must hurt but there's no pain and I'm tossed breathless within skriking split of scream. 'You can't do this to me again, what have I done to you, what have I done? Please make him be alright, please!'

Our Paul's fallen. Not sure what that means. It means

looking after my mother, it means something to do with Jimmy, but what does that *mean*? In the epicentre of all this cascading collision there's an impossible thought, an impossible feeling. Has another brother died? Another gone?

This instantly erupting madness is the first I remember of it, but there must have been people telling her what's happened. Whom, I don't know. Just recall detonation, flashpoint, then caught in the *kaboom* and playing dead of it all. Something was instantly emergency; there was noise, panicked rush, running out, slamming doors and splintering clash of emotion. Whatever happened it was too fast, blurred and within it all a horribly dawning recognition. Our Paul can't be gone... he takes me to New Brighton, Southport, tells me jokes, buys me sweets, he nicknamed Little John Zooney off *Fireball XL5*, called him Jai from *Tarzan* – and he's right, Little John's spittin' image of them both. When I'm at school he takes Little John to New Brighton, Southport, and because he used to take me I get jealous of that. He's funny, dangerous, calls Little John Scone-'ead, generous, acrobatic and, like Captain Scarlet, indestructible. This can't be like Jimmy; he can't be dead like him.

'Oh Lord, please, please not again, not again!' May is so much desperate noise and I'm being held under, released and drowning in wailing swamp of yell. There's welcome space then once again her noise fills my body, my head. Not sure I pass out, but know I'm sometimes not here, gone; there's a belt of blackness, then back. Although on repeat, everything's weirdly new. Seems there's millions of ways to tumble and squash, a million more ways to hear screaming. My right ear is jammed against the howl of grief, I hear its clawing battering bass, feel the terrified tremble of its wounded animal. I don't know what it's like for a mother to lose a child and thankfully never will, but sure as hell know how it sounds. I'm frightened but have to stay still. All I'm able to do. Suddenly my head's in a corner of chair I've not experienced before, but I know every inch of this chair; this is my watching the telly, playing with her pinny-strings, *Pogles' Wood* and *The Avengers* chair. Forehead slides from faux leather and I'm sat bolt upright on her knee, her head dead-weight thumps my shoulder and noise of sobbing earthquakes. There's no witch, no Mrs Peel, just my face a cheek away from hers, a breath away from lips agony-yelping, 'You can't do this to me Lord, not again, not again, take me take me!' I reach to hold her and my head thuds the arm of chair. I know but don't know where I am, I don't know I'm here because here's not here anymore, not home. It's me and my mother, nightmare wrestling, Jackie Pallo, four-armed smash, ten, nine, eight, submit, in out, in out, shaken all about, a macabre twisting on the ropes hokey-cokey. Our Paul used to take me looking for bommy wood, him and our Chris. He was more games than our Chris, more play and more importantly more pocket money. Our Paul told me Paul Street was named after him and I told everybody Paul Street was named after our Paul. Recently scolded me when he thought I was to blame for getting our Little John run over by a car.

May's making sounds like he's dead, gone and never coming back. I know these noises; sounds like she's summoning death. Slamming her hand into my back she holds me to her shoulder. Something of her feels defeated. The *can't take any more of this* conquers, desperation's won, there's a sense she's slipping from me, perhaps unconsciousness, perhaps death, we're a tree, forest, falling...

'Ma, Ma, he's aright, he's gonna be okay!'

'What lad, what, what's up, what's gone on at the hospital?'

I'm thrown to the back of our chair; relief of it instantly amazing. I can move all by myself, wave my arms, I'm me again. I don't know which of my brothers it is, but his obvious physical/vocal elation is immediately relieving and what he's saying, life-saving. In a split-but-still-panicked second something feels over, passed, gone. May looks up to The Sacred

Heart, 'Thank you Lord, thank you, thank you!' I know our Paul's alive.

Not sure if 6A's actually full but there's so much partying emotion around it feels chocker. For the first time in what seems forever there's the unmistakable thrill of togethering celebration. There must be ale – always is at times like this – but it's far more than a partying-before-the-pubs do. It's not the massive noise of a winning goal being scored by either The Reds or The Blues, but it's very much the same elated atmosphere of victory. There's a lot of instant hugging and necessary laughter, feeling like a memory come to life. This is how it used to be, what we were; alive, busying and animated, our bodies filling the room with elbow-angled, dancing brio. People pour through our kitchen door bringing with them that same upbeat sense of goal-scoring. It's the noise of a brother not being dead. The brand new sound of survival.

Although words differ, all this nattering conversation's the same and I'm starting to slowly make out what's just happened. Our Paul had been working at a huge docklands warehouse and fell from the very top of it. It was much higher than Jimmy but, thank God, he didn't die. His fall fortuitously broken by a lorry load of empty tea chests. There are horror stories it might have been either driving in or away from the courtyard and it caught him just in the nick of time. Those horror stories could have validity, but Scousers do love to further adventure and dangerously embellish an already terrifying tale. Whatever might or not be being added on, the bulk of it was true.

I'm sat behind my mother and people are reaching down to her as she's reaching out. The women around her are doing that psychic *no words, just looks* thing again and I swear I can hear what they're not saying. They've half-circled around the back our chair and I can feel the metaphysical outreach of their love. A kind of forcefield covers May, invisible to the naked eye but warm and real as a pan of scouse. Our Paul's mates are visibly shaking with joy, smiles on their faces mean a jibbering-jabbering everything. I see my brothers together, Big John, our Thomas and Chris; they're what/who they used to be, completely and happily connected. I know our Paul can't be here because he's getting better in 'ozzy (Scouse for 'hospital'), but do miss our Jimmy. I clock their shoulder-jigging shadows on our wall and one's missing. Since Jimmy's death this is the first time my brothers have looked like they've something wonderful in common. They seem so happy together and I profoundly know they're my family. As much as I love everyone around, once again it's getting too adult conversational and time for me to wander. I shove 'n' shift through them. My hair is hundreds-times hurriedly scuffed, my head hundreds-times patted, shoulders hundreds-times shook, but right now I need the wideness of outside.

Tiptoe-peering over the ledge of our landing and that's all I want. The noise from 6A is booming out our front door, an invisible giant's intangible hand is trying its best to grab and pull me back in. Other people are running up the landing toward me, big beaming faces zoom into mine, one of them jokingly biting my nose. Again, an obligatory hair-shake and celebratory fist-clenched shoulder-jabs of *gerrinthere Gerrid lad!* Even though they can't talk back, I'm sure those Blackstock Gardens chimneys opposite are congratulating me too, telling me in chimney to *gerrinthere*.

Suddenly everything's too much and I'm breathing heavily, ribs of my body rhythmically banging the wall I'm leaning on. My head's plagued by our Paul nearly dying, his face flashing off 'n' on. What would it mean if he had died and what would we do, how on this stupid Earth would we have taken it? Catching my breath, profusely sweating, can't rid my mind of the worst. The noise of everything's disappeared and it's just me inside myself. As reluctant a babysitter as he was, as rough 'n' tumble as it brilliantly was, our Paul Butler brought me up. What would my world be like if he wasn't in it, what would I do, who would I be and where would I go? Feels like I'll never be able to properly breathe again and my sobbing's becoming too helplessly noisy. No one can see me like this, promised me Nin. I keep my promise and somehow manage to walk away. I'm all-fours crawling to the top landing and I sit, arms-around-knees huddled on the final step. An ointment dim of golden light instantly soothes. I feel cave-like bathed in honeyed salve and am calming. What is it about these grey stairs, this red brick arched cavern, this bandaging faded light? Why does it all somehow feel a comforting, wraparound, kiss-on-the-forehead parental?

It's just a few days and he hobbles in on crutches. There's an almighty cheer and I can't believe he's in front of me; our Paul is back. It's a bit like when he came home from Borstal, but much more emotional and this time we're instantly partying. He immediately looks stunned; it might be too much for him, but he's a Butler so it soon turns into a joke. Something to do with Long John Silver and *ah ha me'heartys*. But I don't care about laughing, I'm just knocked out to see him. Don't readily remember this, but grew up constantly told I was hugging him so much they couldn't get me off him, and there's no doubt I am now. He's got stitches in his head, all up his leg, and no sooner has he settled down than he's showing off his scars. Our Chris calls him Frankenstein. Ordinarily our Paul adored being centre stage, craved it, but I can see a kind of hesitance; how someone still in shock might look and perhaps that's why I won't let him go (God, me Nin taught me well). Paul's a slightly startled wide-eyed by all the emotionally charged bravado, but we'd just lost a brother from falling and one's just survived, so all we can do is cheer. May's smiling and quietly staring at him. There's so much maternal love in all she is, we all feel it and hug her. She gets up to make Paul something to eat. Even in her oil-cloth scraping shuffle there's a fluffy be-slipper'd skip, and no sooner up, she's back again with a leaning tower of boiled ham sandwiches.

Paul's mates roar in with a *go 'ed, Buck la, fuckin' gear y'back!* 6A is full as it's ever been and it seems everyone is jigging around my stitched-up brother. There's a sense we're all in on this huge slice of place and knowledge. *Two of them falling in such a short space of time and one survives, what's the fuckin' chances of that?* seems to be the conversational vibe. It's mixed with such festive reverie but there's a silenced sense, especially with a still-grieving family, that far too much has happened. We simply didn't have the words, but what we can't say we show.

Bizarre it takes the near death of one brother to survive the real death of another, but a slyboots-something about that's worked. Something about all of this is once again the family we always were. Not saying our Jimmy's in any way forgotten or tossed aside, quite the contrary, with some people even suggesting it was the ghost of Jimmy saving Paul's life. It's just once again my family are covered in the unique camaraderies and confidently blasting bravados of who we are, what we *always were*.

It's a fantastic do, but I hear somewhere through it, someone saying to me Ma… 'Told ye he'd be alright didn't I May, what did I say girl? Lightnin' never strikes twice.'

XIII
Judy Garland is my Spirit Animal

'Gerrid, Gerrid, c'mon wake up kid, time to go.'

Russ Tamblyn's *Tom Thumb* didn't cut the mustard; apparently fifteen minutes in I fell fast asleep. Judy Garland in *The Wizard of Oz* on the other hand, had me on my seat bouncing up 'n' down like a cartoon jack-in-the-box on exceptionally good E.

Our Thomas and Angela had taken me out, I think to experience some ordinary, upbeat, kid stuff. Life at 6A had been pretty chaotic, so they must have thought all the sweets I could eat, an onion-swamped hotdog, Dorothy 'n' Toto would be much welcome respite. I was a virgin to the pictures and the first movie I ever saw at a cinema has historically made more people gay than sequins. I revelled in every bright gaudy second of that movie and wildly cheered when it returned to monochromatic homeliness.

We're in the ABC picture house next door to Blackler's departmental store. Remember thinking inside of it looked exactly the same as that phoney Wizard's gaff in Oz. I'm not used to this kind of grandly lit opulence and initially find the ballroom-sized etiquette of cinema completely mind-blowing. Sinking into the plush pile of its footstep-muffling carpet is like walking on marshmallowing silence, and the ear-blasting, head-dancing, jazz-stabbing staccato of the Pearl & Dean adverts as much pneumatic drilling as music. Usherettes, torch-lit from underneath, seem even more wondrously cheekbone/ lipstick-glamorous as anything on the big screen. I remember clocking their choc ices, ciggies, boxes of Maltesers, Bryant and May matches, all lying down together in the same tray and wondering how they fit them all in, then asking myself if these exotically dressed usherettes are recently released genies. They certainly look like them; maybe their bottles are behind the screen. Everything around me's eclectically enchanting, whilst at the same time slightly misty and surreally becalming. It's so many enormous things and from the off I'm wide-eyed overwhelmed by its fabulous rising/falling, festoon-flouncing, theatrically-ruched curtains. Love the house-lights dimming from a hard pink pastel and, before the delicious weave of blackout, hearing that instantly quieting hit; feels like church if Mass were a Burlesque strip show. Then a gingham-pinafored Judy sings to a flea-bitten mutt in Kansas and nothing has ever felt more pictures perfect. If any motion picture could change a kid's imaginative landscape it's this one... don't think I'm in Liverpool anymore. However, its double-bill partner fails to in any way reach and off I jolly well snooze.

Wait a minute, was I just in that movie I woke up from, was all this in my dream? Being shook awake and picked up by our Tommy's a comforting, natural sensation; a slight fuzzing start then instant, arms-reaching recognition. No sooner up 'n' about than I find myself twisted up upon his shoulders and it feels just like home. I've recently been told by my brand new bezzy there's no place like it and I haven't have to click my heels together three times to get there.

Liverpool city centre's night-time shining and, like Oz with Dorothy, I'm suddenly spun from something then plonked in the all-important middle of somewhere else. Perhaps because my head is now chock-a-block full of yellow brick roads, witches, wizards 'n' towering Emerald vistas, my own city centre feels just that bit more Cinemascope 'n' Technicolor. Living so near we walk home, my eyes an enlivened-popping by so much garishly sassy, gaslit lightening. Opposite Lime Street Station a row of buildings is lit full of neon-shimmering commercial brands; Guinness, Double Diamond and Schweppes, those much-drunk bottled bevvies, centre-stage stars of this free-for-the-public light show. There's something particularly engaging about that off/on, bright red, flashing Double Diamond sign; seems to hypnotically draw me in like it may be a portal to another world or, much better still, another time.

Carried by our Tommy, Angela at his side, gnawing a gobful of chewy sweets and suddenly, as if by magic, the whole wide world's alright with me. There are flickering snippets of joy impossible to write, paint, sculpt or in any way fully describe, because they're beyond art, clay, literature. Perhaps not even memory, just tightly held wisps of euphoric feeling buried deep in the mushy bloods of marrow, the memory of memory. Can feel electric caresses of blurring neon on my big-smile face, light's lightly kissing my cheeks, sense the speed of my mousy-haired head spinning so's not to miss a single second of whatever's glittering about me. I'm floating in the musically breathable air of everything and, in this tiny twister of perfection, high as a two-worlds-connecting rainbow. I've just this evening gotten myself a brand new noggin alive with Scarecrow-possibility, Tin-Man-endeavouring and Cowardly-Lion-hilarity. That, and I'm bobbing along on my big brother's shoulders, my hands tightly clasped under our Tommy's chin, my juddering chin atop his head. He jogs on the spot so my head judders that little bit more and all three of us are laughing. A forever memory a breath and thought away; a slightly un-touchable top-of-the-world, on-the-shoulders-of-giants feeling.

We go the Scottie Road way home and, separating Scotland Road from Bevington Bush, pass the enormous mystery and majesty of Arden House (well, I say mystery and majesty because I'm completely off my head on Oz's glistening Emerald City). This monstrous, red brick brute of a monument, now home to The Salvation Army, once shelter for returning seamen then for drunks 'n' vagrants, silhouettes a Chateaux Dracula-spectacular. Now, because I thought tramps could be God, I was madly fascinated by Arden House. Who knows, maybe God was actually in there, supping meth, farting, pissing the bed, quaking through night terrors or slobber-snoring past himself. Also, for some sinister, murkier reasons, and nefariously something to do with the docks, there are tonnes of massively long lorries parked outside 'n' around it. A scurrilous undercurrent surrounds these parked vehicles, almost certainly involving some sort of covert criminality and (I think now) prostitution. I can unclearly see bobbing, skulking heads and garbled-hear harsh-whispered hisses; it's completely gripping. But I'm atop of my big, dead-'ard brother, so nothing or no one can get me – not even a screeching flock of bat-winged demon monkeys.

Ooh, it seems after Dorothy and Oz every enog is filled with potential adventure. I'm put down by Boroughs Baths, very near my old infant school, St. Brigid's, and there ahead, right in front of me, I see it: my very own Yellow Brick Road. In truth, it's just slate-grey cobbled Blackstock Street, but after that film everywhere has become somewhere else. We pass The Littley (Scouse for 'the little square'), the smallest of the three red brick bouquets making up Blackstock Gardens and, being of a more diminutive scale, the cosiest looking of the three living areas. I loved The Littley; it housed Mary Mac's sisters Kathleen Flood, Margey Murphy and Irene Edwards, and Little John, Stephen and I were always playing out with their kids. Because watching *The Wizard of Oz* was like taking two tabs of LSD, The Littley now double-drop shines like an illegally raving Brigadoon. Tonight, The Littley is lit a multi-hued kaleidoscopic and golden night-kissed on the lips by the transportive magic of hallucinogenic cinema.

Because of so much robbery and so many factories easily robbed, there'd often be heavily overcoat'd men stood outside around fiery braziers guarding them. We called these balaclava'd, fingerless-gloved old blokes *cockywatchmen*. They were incredibly friendly wrinkle-faced men who gave us sweets – and we did take them off them, though more Everton Mints 'n' humbugs than anything too fancy. Standing sentinel above their flame-torching gateways and protecting their all-important castles, and because I'm all Glinda-the-Good-Witch'd-up on meself, they look like mythic gargoyles. Even the soft, red-glassed glow of yellow Corporation oil lamps hung around that-day-dug holes shine like fulsome fireflies; stocky, little, rouge-bruised fairies, confidently reeking of City Council-soaked petroleum. Circling the tops of Blackstock Street's streetlights appear to be golden spectral orbs which could well be full of wide-smiled, wand-waving good witches. Or maybe the wayward, beleaguered souls of long-sung, drunken ancestors, finally finding their ways home.

This collage of tumbling imagery feels like mine. I belong here. And here, this Scouse Kansas, full to brimming with colluding illusion, is my own backyard. I try doing the skipping Yellow Brick Road routine down Blackstock Street only to slip onto its bumpy moist cobbles. Laughing, our Tommy runs to get me and no sooner on the floor than I'm flown back onto his shoulders. Still laughing, he calls me a little tit-'ead and I couldn't love him more. We all make our not-skipping but giggling way to 6A, where May is more than delighted to see us, especially me. Always a worrier but now, after Jimmy 'n' Paul, she's much worse. If any one of us is out of her sights for any length of time she immediately thinks we're dead. Tommy, instantly noticing her anxiety, pipes up, 'Can't believe he fell asleep through *Tom Thumb*, Ma. Couldn't keep him fuckin' still through *The Wizard of Oz* could we Angela? Like he 'ad worms.' Although laughing, May's holding me tight and I'm taken out of the spell; Glinda's gone. I squeeze my way through her to the back of our chair and with my chin on her shaking shoulder, she calms.

It's just the four of us, a real fire, toast and cups of tea.

Angela tells May how taken I was by Judy Garland. May replies with, 'She was always a favourite of mine girl, no one like 'er. Shame wha' 'appened to 'er eh. When there's a Judy Garland film on telly we always watch, don't we Gerrid?' With a head full of chorusing Dorothy Gales, I nod *yes*. Love it to bits when all the family are gathered, but also cherish these smaller more intimate pow-wows; too many half-pissed brothers in the room and it can get competitively rowdy. Just one of them, especially if with a wife or girlfriend, and feels like more can be said and understood.

Tommy and Angela get set to leave; probably going for a couple of drinks then back to the Hollywoods'. On their way out 'n' on the sly, our Tommy's picks up a scraggy arl monkey toy of mine and, from behind the kitchen door, makes the screeching noise of one of the Wicked Witch of the West's bat-winged demon apes. 'Remember this tonight Gerrid. Y'fuckin' shit yerself!' Of course I remember, but too busy laughing to answer. He's done this party trick before, to me, Little John and Stephen sat on the couch. Tonight though, it's different and a bit more magic; it's about what we three have just witnessed.

May's tightening up, disappearing, but right now and for the first time that doesn't matter. I'm deffo telling her what happened and how beautiful it was. She can drift off to wherever she needs to go; I got all that a while back. But wherever she is, this evening, I've been to Oz and never gonna shut up about my new friend, Dorothy.

Something remarkable had happened and I was forever changed. I was well used to magical storytelling but another notion was cemented that night. May was right, we were televisually mainline addicted to *The Harvey Girls* 'n' *Meet Me in St. Louis*, and would religiously watch Judy whenever she was on TV. Our telly was a distant, small, black 'n' white box, often going out and sometimes we didn't have a silver shilling to put it back on again. That night I realised we didn't have to depend on little coins from me Ma's purse to complete the silver screen movie. That night I realised there are big, glittering places, where puny silver shillings didn't matter. Huge, colourful, palatial places for people like us, taking us to other worlds where dreams are truth. I had always kinda suspected, but that night was proved right: there's magic absolutely everywhere.

XIV
Unlucky Strike

The raucously-pitched, night-time noises from my brothers' bedroom were wild, the best kind of wildness; speedy, manic laughter and endless, jibing, bantering wild. Nine times out of ten May wouldn't go to bed until the lads got home and when the lads did get home they were usually pissed out of their brains. Tommy, Chris 'n' Paul slept in the same room and often at weekends they'd have their mates stay over. I'd be in bed with me Ma and we'd hear it. It'd normally start off with a kind of mannish giggling before manically erupting into a full-on hysterical party. Completely annoying May and throwing her fluffy slipper to the wall, she'd yell, 'Shut the fuck up will y'z, we're trying to get to sleep in 'ere!' Of course, with it being a fluffy slipper, it made no impacting noise whatsoever. I, on the other hand, loved every out-there, big-ballsy-banging nuance of it.

Scousers are a complex yet simple breed; believe me, no one does anger and fighting with more fist-punching accuracy (except perhaps Glaswegians), but we're also completely addicted to insanely noisy joy. Not just laughter for the sake of laughter, but the visible/vocal reliving of event and re-augmenting of story. A Scouser doesn't simply tell you what's happened; they'll do their animated best to almost psychically transfer whatever experience they've had into your physical body. A firing-on-all-syllables generous narcissism which is all about the *me me me* showtime of the storyteller – but said storyteller will have failed miserably if they haven't generously given you every delicious ingredient of the tale.

The lads would do exactly that. An out-of-all-control frenzy of description, a bombardment of so much overlapping sound, uniquely employing a surreal use of language which can only be truly understood if sharing the same locality. I wouldn't know the rapping velocity of every machine-gunning word they'd be shooting off, but did know some, and excitedly knew when all growed-up I'd know them all. It was that stomach buzzing/churning feeling I loved most, that one year soon I'd be doing what my brothers did. Watching them weekend-disappear into town was weekly-mesmerising. They brazenly looked like they were entering somewhere/something just a few steps away remarkable. At night, their town must be as glittery, mythically shining as Dorothy's Oz.

Stood in my brothers' bedroom and above me women on chairs are hanging up large white sheets. They could be family, maybe neighbours, or perhaps they're *the women of the parish*. The women of the parish are a group attached to Our Lady's of Ascension who, when things urgently need doing, will some-times and more often not most times, do them. If it is indeed them, then they've moved my brothers' single beds into our broken-bikes 'n' junk-filled spare room.

I'm a bit lost 'n' confused by it all because if they are the women of the parish then they often come to help when somebody's died. They're making everything in here look like heaven and, although not yet completely heavenly, I can still see slithers of wallpaper. There's an eerie calm starting to sneakily-surround and it's beginning to feel more than a little bit holy. I'm faintly reminded of sitting on a church bench before taking my first confession. Not thinking just looking, not looking just being, because that's all I'm able to do. There's an animated something about their expert toing/froing I'm finding picturesquely soothing; they look like a cartoon ballet. I'm unable to work out their now grey, smudged faces and can't quite tell if they look sad, but misery is everywhere and much of it's physically emanating from them. Bodies move a stoically damp, almost elegantly sad; only recently seen them do it and these bodies sense a similar smooth weighty, drenched. These women inhabit the same morbidly slow/fast plodding pace as each other. It's as if they've no idea where they're going then suddenly snap bolt alert, knowing exactly where need to be. Sad bodies instinctively know what chair to step on, what white drape to tack up. Sad hands know how to expertly take those tacks from sad mouths.

There's too much noise outside of here and I don't want to hear it. Whoever these women, they're caring and literally changing the space. It now feels like somewhere else and right now somewhere else is exactly where I want to be. Really big men in black suits arrive; they disturb everything and look oddly misplaced, scuffling about like bumbling, clumsy shadows. They first-name-know the women and there's talking. A perturbing sense of disbelief's everywhere, especially within conversation, and one of the men actually says, 'How fuckin' unbelievable's all this!' One of the women replies, 'I know lad, poor May eh, what must she be goin' through? God bless 'er.' The suited men are carrying large letter-A-shaped pieces of wood. By now, the women have covered the bedroom window with white silken cloth. A little away from each other the A-shaped pieces of wood are placed under the window. Instantly glowing a celestial luminous, there's now a rectangle of curtained bright where our window used to be. Hung opposite, slightly lit by its shimmer, a large 'n' imposing dark wooden crucifix. In the middle of the room resides the dramatic finishing touch: a giant golden candlestick with a thick cream-coloured church candle and, as if from nowhere, a brand new scent of incense. My brothers' untidy/ungodly bedroom normally smelt of nicotine, farts and stale ale, but now I'm miraculously standing in the centre of a beautifully illuminated, mysteriously fragrant slice of afterlife. Whatever spell this secretive Catholic coven's cast has worked; they've made my brothers' bedroom appear paradisaically empyrean.

To my surprise, I'm suddenly alone; those generously busying bustlers have vanished. I'm feeling calmly in tune with the enveloping quiet they've created when, outside, there's an even bigger sense of audibly clashing commotion. One of my brothers pops his head round the door, angrily telling me to get out. I don't want to, it's safer here, but he's my big brother, so I have to. It takes less than a second to step from heaven into hell. Struggling to carry a long pine box, enormous, monstering silhouettes are at our front door. The box seems incredibly heavy and something about all of this insanity has shrunk our doorway, making it look like a tiny oblong of light. Shadowy, shifting shoulders are shuffling toward me and in the hands of those massive shifting shoulders rests the wide head of the wooden box. The other big silhouette is clumsily negotiating the thinner foot of it. The wooden box bangs into corners of wall and, like a cumbersome wardrobe might, has to be held high, lifted and strategically angled. The noise of sobbing and wailing builds a maddening cacophonous and everything around me is wrong. It's all piling up, horribly crowding, closing in and, just like our telly, my head goes out.

6th of October 1970, six weeks after our Paul's fall, little less than four months after our Jimmy's fatal accident, and Thomas Butler is dead. Once again, he died falling, although unlike our Paul, who fell the highest and survived, he tumbled from a nine-foot piece of scaffolding and didn't.

What is it about these few months and falling? Why is it happening to us? Because so much of our Tommy's death has left me, I'm not even sure I thought that. I recall a few things but any sense of a normal timeline has long gone. Whatever's left mostly fractious moments, strobing an on/off insane impossible.

Unending, echoing hollowness and heartbreaking storms of disbelief dark-cloud everything. There's a sound to this kind of weather, oddly intrusive 'n' loud; a negative noise, a un-noise, a once was but now not there noise. I think of them as the sounds of grief. I still hear it, it's part of who I am. For me it's forever young and confused; makes me feel a million miles away from everybody. It's a creeping sense of unfair abandon-ment slowly tiptoeing toward me then... suddenly engulfs 'n' swamps. I'm now in my sixties and that cloying swamp monster still feels like its drowning an eight-year-old me. Just realised, I had my eighth birthday in between all this and have no memory of it whatsoever.

My family was built off the beaten track. Wonky balancing on its wrong sides, our historic foundations were always more than a little rocky. What's left of its building blocks, its red brick certainties, were being brutally removed by the cruellest game of Jenga, but with brothers. (It's funny, I've always thought that game's oblongs of wood appear like skinny coffins.) However dysfunctional we were never really seemed to matter because everyone around 'n' about us was in some way similar. Lots of families had difficulties and we were, on occasion, invited into those difficulties; the blessing or perhaps curse of such tightly close-knit communities. What was happening to us was different to the normality of shared dysfunction because death, particularly multiple young death, impacts on family so personally. We were always bonded; for all our hard-nosed, ramshackle bravura we were an incredibly close familial unit. But this four-month series of cataclysmic events had eroded, chipped away, gnarled and distorted us: you've not only lost your dead brothers, but the still-alive ones too. They can somehow surface-bravado the same, but because you know *it* – and it's a complex *it* – they know you know *it* and that *it* stays a psychically-communicated silent. In the same room but not in the same room. Looking out of the same windows but seeing differing vistas. We were being pulled away from one another, but there was an uncertain, colluding *something* about that weird sense of distancing, paradoxically, further connecting. We were hurting and knew sometimes that's all it can be; that pain's ours, my pain's mine and their pain theirs. It's a multi-corridor'd void a million miles wide and all's a trippy, crumbling, kaleidoscopic white.

Our Tommy died the day before his birthday; never quite made it to twenty-two. It's bizarre, but when I think of him 'n' Jimmy they're still tall, wide and old. At twenty-one and twenty-nine they seem much older than me at sixty. When I think of their authority and how they filled the room with personality, it doesn't feel in their twenties. I was a skinny, camp thing, a light, bright, flamingo feather, so always being lifted up and carried. They were never gentle about lifting me, it was forever a bit haphazardly butch, but what I remember most is complete trust; I knew they'd never drop me. It's not just about being carried, it's also about being taught. Something about trust like that immediately becomes who you are, forming your juvenile personality and the protective love, acrobatically inherent, forever inhabits. I know I'm a big grown-up man now, but in recall they're gregariously huge and I'm always a just-lifted, excitable, tiny kid, giggling away. I'm Jelly Beans.

Auntie Mary, my mother's oldest sister, and Auntie Fanny, my dad's sister, are sat with May. Auntie Mary has an earthy, keen, intelligent demeanour, whilst Auntie Fanny is straight-backed, immaculately quaffed and sternly glamorous. Both are aesthetically different looking women but class colours them similar. My aunties are on the couch and May is collapsed on her chair. There's no sound but it's deafening and, although they're most certainly in our kitchen, I know it's the void.

Cousin Peter Butler's tall, jam-packed with infectious humour; a bit like Big John, one of those Scousers immediately lighting up a room and always noticed. Our kitchen's once again full and I'm not in a good way. I'm probably trying to disguise it. Why, I don't know, but it's what I always did 'n' still do. Peter's been doing this for the past couple of days now but, like a brother once might have, he sees and immediately lifts me up. His is a remarkably soothing demeanour, voice upbeat and warm, with a boisterously healing way about him. Today's Peter Butler is showing me how to box. He reminds me of our Tommy and, exactly like with our Tommy, I half-arse pretend I'm taking it in. I know Peter's protecting me; sees my surface grief, one of very few adults who do. He's trying his level best to reassure and doing a fantastic job.

My immediate family are still incredibly hurt about Jimmy and because of Thomas now irreparably devastated. Not saying they don't see me; they do. After all, we share that *it*, but something about them, about *me*, isn't here right now. Because May is broken and my brothers always drunk, some of the time I can't help feeling invisible. I don't think they know how much I'm hurting but how could they when, right in front of them, their present familial histories are being so cruelly erased.

Peter says he's going in to see our Tommy and do I want to go with him. He kindly insists I don't have to, but because I don't want to be put down, don't want to disappear, I reply *yes*. We weave from the kitchen toward my brother's bedroom and I love being held high above so many people's heads. I'm treating it like a game and it's making me feel a tiny bit powerful. Our small hallway is also full of people and I annoyingly tap the tops of their heads like a miniscule Pope anointing them with chocolate covered fingers.

I've not been in the room since the coffin arrived and am immediately re-struck by how mythically white it all is. As we step from our dark scruffy hallway into a bright alien world, I see his coffin and immediately feel sick. It only takes a second to reach his casket but it drags an age; I'm not ready.

'God, he looks so handsome doesn't he Gerrid? Us Butlers

are a good lookin' lot.' Peter's trying to stay upbeat but I sense a vocal crack. 'Y'poor Ma shouldn't have to be goin' through this lad.' I look down and our Tommy's like Nin's holy statues; half-smiling, his skin a waxy pallid, his eyes closed but not sleeping. He's deffo there in front of me but gone. Where to though, and like Jimmy, I've no idea. Perhaps they're nowhere together. There's a disturbing stillness about all of this, as if silence could punch. Tommy should be up 'n' about, joking. He should be taking Peter's boxing duties offa him and teaching me himself. If he gets up now, I'll promise him to take it more seriously this time. I won't giggle; he wanted me to box, kept telling me. He, more than anyone else, wanted me to learn to look after myself. He's all in white surrounded by his birthday cards and they look lovely, like little story books. I suddenly remember the size of that giant rust-coloured ten bob note, how it impressed my mates, the flaring, flashing neons, Angela and Dorothy. Our Tommy could bend red hot pokers with his bare hands, get me Ma out the house; he was great at impossible things. He can't just be lying there. If the ghost of Jimmy saved our Paul's life, why didn't he save Tommy's?

'C'mon Tommy lad, time to wake up, wake up now.' Our Chris forcefully bombards toward the coffin; he's drunk and deranged. 'C'mon lad, c'mon now, wake up will ye, time to get up, wake the fuck up will ye!' Peter asks him to calm down. He doesn't and can't. 'Why won't you wake up? C'mon Tommy, wake up!' Chris physically rocks the coffin then grabs our Tommy's face, pulling at it, and through fleshy contortion I see the mortician's stitches stretch in his lips and eyes; if Chris pulls any harder they'll snap. I snap. *I'm gonna die tomorrow, we all are, and I'm to blame for all of this, it's my fault.* It's hardly seconds but those thoughts flash on 'n' off forever. I'm quickly put down and Peter attends to our now-bawling Chris, pulling him away from the coffin and soothing him. From the bedroom I run into the hallway and there's our Tommy's best mate. He's a big hard man, a bouncer, wide-shouldered 'n' strong, but now he's falling into a wall, being swallowed by it and screaming on repeat, 'Not Tommy, no not Tommy. It can't be, it can't be.' Through our kitchen door I see May leaning on the arm of her chair. She's a too-shook grey and staring at the noise, her hollow eyes a widened blank, a ghost. I fall backwards, hoping to spill into my desert; it's where I've been going to when things get crazy. I can feel it there, wide-open, sunny and warm, with just me in the centre. Sometimes it's a spaceship, sometimes it's nowhere, but normally and preferably it's my own private desert. I'm strobing in 'n' out of it but too many voices are trying to get in, asking me if I'm alright. I want them to shut up, this is my desert, not theirs, they're not allowed. I'm back and look up to see our Paul 'n' Chris; they're screaming at each other and fist-fighting. I'm in 'n' out, blurring between worlds and running away.

Sitting under the giant arch connecting Blackstock Street to our other big square is where I once again land. I'm cold, it's wet and exactly where I want to be. Perhaps this is my desert in red brick autumnal form. I'm an exhausted frightened, the panic of me going to die tomorrow in every cell of my body, and completely convinced I just witnessed the world end. Not sure if it is dark, but we're in October so could well be. I feel overwhelmingly responsible, thinking that if at some point I'd have just done something different this wouldn't be happening and which brother am I gonna kill next. Well, tomorrow I'll stop killing them because it'll be me dead.

From that day to now, I've never had any sense of longevity. I'm actually amazed to be sitting here typing this. Although still murkily lurking, the extreme panic of me dying tomorrow has long since calmed. Y'know, there's a bit of a get out clause with that rather grim scenario: as Little Orphan Annie's song states, tomorrow is only a day away, therefore *always* a day away. So, who knows, perhaps I got it wrong and am in fact immortal. Seriously, it panicked the crap outta me for years and the crow-cloaked, bastard spectre of it still ill-lingers. One of these days I am going to die tomorrow and next day, as always, the sun will still come out.

But I can't leave my desert and return to 6A; it's all far too much. Anyway, there's something about being this emotionally heightened making everything look decoratively different. I've my microscopic super-vision back, can see rock fall on halfies. For now, I'll look to the same walls, walk the same streets and, like my best pal Dorothy, magic myself somewhere else. I'm getting really good at that.

Along our landing to the stairwell, the three brothers I have left and three others are shoulders-carrying our Thomas's coffin. Everywhere's thick cotton black, hatted and veiled. I'm wearing a tie, my first time; I had a dickie-bow for my Communion. Thomas's fiancée, Angela, is covered in that same dark light Janet 'n' me Ma were, sitting on and around her shoulders like a too-heavy stole. My mother's just hopeless noise in a scrunched-up ball; I can hear her inside our flat, sobbing.

I turn my head, look over the landing, and our big square's chocker. Everybody's dotted everywhere. Some people are on their parts of the landings staring over and down and the entire world's looking at us. I like it; makes me feel special. We're Blackstock Gardens' superstars and a part of me will always want this. I'm held into a lot of walking legs, a series of different hands rubbing my back and head. I'm visible today and belong to this. It's all incredibly slow and everyone instinctively knows not to hurry. We emerge from our ground-floor stairwell; the weeping is a bellowing choral and head-scarf'd women hold hankies to air-catching mouths. Some people are huddled together, others a foot-from-foot-shuffling alone, but they're all there for us. I hear someone say *those Butlers, like the fuckin' Scouse Kennedys*. I don't know what it means but because it makes Big John laugh, so do I. In a very few steps and taking our time, we follow Thomas's coffin to the waiting hearse and cars. On route, among the many floral wreathes, I spy a chair made from flowers. I ask what it's for and am gently told it's for Tommy; apparently it's a vacant chair where the dead once sat. Looks to me like it's floating above the other more ordinary, less glamorous wreaths, and I imagine it a lot more than a fancy floral tribute. I instantly believe it's crafted from fairytales; a story chair. People are smoking and there's a distinct scent of booze. Last night was the all-night vigil before the funeral so everybody stayed up late and drank. It was the first time I ever saw bottles of whiskey in the house 'n' there were lots of them; it's what's done. Everyone's eyes are beaten, defeated, red-raw and robbed of rest. They place our Tommy's casket into the long-windowed front car; we all lovingly look to it then sunken-blunder into ours. Although they're sat down in this limousine, my brothers seem somehow taller and, in this saddest of moments, they've never looked more like each other. They're mumble-talking in the secret language of whispered big brother that I don't quite understand. That's okay, today I don't want to. I look to our Rosary-tinted windows, at so many beads being thumbed, pressed away from each other and reflected upon, and behind those beads glimpse the saddest faces. These people don't want this to be happening to us.

We sit on the front bench of the church. Above us, Jesus is gigantic in dying. We're all being crucified right now and his wide-armed, doomy looming makes perfect sense: he's narrating the story. I love it in Our Lady's; we've stopped being superstars, just family now. We're in-time head-bowed, sat, kneeling and stood together. So, this is what funerals look like from the inside.

The journey from Our Lady's, Eldon Street to Ford Cemetery seems to take forever. Deffo the longest I've ever been in a car. When we get there, we follow Thomas's coffin to its home, a newly dug hole in the ground which we gather around. He's in the ground now, they used ropes to lower him there. It was our Janet's plot and she's given it over to my family. I'm told our Jimmy's down there too and think *oh so that's where he went,*

doesn't look much like heaven, not anything like our Tommy's bedroom.
I'm immediately aware they're now on top of each other.
There's priest talk and sobbing, priest talk and sobbing, priest
talk and sobbing. He shakes what looks like a horse's tail of
water over the coffin. Not sure if it's raining but feels like it is.
Out of nowhere a shovel of earth is placed under my chin; it
smells heavy. Our Paul tells me to grab a handful and throw it
onto the lid of our Tommy's new home. I like that it's clammy
clay, thick and moist. Feels real and connecting and for a while
I hold on to it. Letting go, it hits the lid of our Tommy's coffin.

It's that damp clod of ground I remember most. I can still
see its definite plummet. I can still hear the fulfilling sound of
its exploding, wood-thudding *splat*. For the first time in a long
time, just for a second, something felt right.

A few years ago, I did a one-off reading of poetry at Liverpool's
Unity Theatre called *Son of Liverpool*. A collection of poems
about my time in my home city, including poems about my
mother and brothers. After the show a big blokey figure came
up to me and said, 'Alright Gerrid lad.' I didn't at first know
who it was until he said, 'It's me soft lad, Ian Hollywood,
Angela's brother.' I then instantly recognised him and immediately apologised for not, saying it was great to see him again.
We feverously started reminiscing and, of course, our Tommy
cropped up. As previously mentioned, Tommy had been staying
at Angela's house a lot and had developed a special big brother
relationship with an eight-year-old Ian – very soon they were
gonna be brothers-in-law. What I found most interesting of all
was Ian telling me that, when Tommy was lying in state in his
bedroom, we'd both been filling balloons with water, then,
from our second-floor landing, laughing and impishly aiming
them at people's heads below. He asked me if I remembered; I
lied and said *yes*. I don't remember. I have no idea of running
around and being a normal, giggling, up-to-no-good eight-
year-old. I clearly must have been though and was incredibly

thankful for the memory. I'm made-up I was still a fuckin' little nuisance. Before my brothers' deaths I recall playing out and scuff-knee'd peskying-about all the time; some of my most cherished memories. With Thomas's death in particular, all I remember is a very little anything or massive strobing trauma. It came as a big heartfelt relief to me to hear I was still doing my level best to piss off adults. Ian then told me the last time he saw our Tommy was when he was leaving the Hollywoods' house for work that morning. Tommy just scuffed Ian's hair and, much like our Jimmy had to me, he said to Ian, 'See y'later kid.' That's all, a simple, friendly, upbeat *see y'later goodbye*. I don't do envy and seriously can't tell you last time I was ever envious. Have to admit though to getting a strangely distant pang of displaced envy when Ian told me that. Not ugly envy, nothing approaching vindictive jealousy, pretty sure it wasn't even adult envy. But I was immediately eight again and wishing it was my head our Tommy had rubbed.

XV
Big Jimmy Butler

There's a passed-down story I can't personally recall about Big Jimmy Butler visiting May at 6A, and to this day I've no idea what he visited for. Apparently, he came in, sat opposite and reached out to toddler me; I ran behind my mother's chair and was, as the tale was so often broadcast, very frightened. I don't remember being a frightened child, wasn't ever told I was, but must have been of my dad. I then crept behind my mother on her chair and, peering over her shoulder, asked who he was. May told me it was my dad and, laughing, added that she'd never seen me look more confused.

Big Jimmy Butler never stopped confusing me and when my brothers died, he broke my heart. But, as well as being a highly qualified heartbreaker (ask me Ma), he was also an actual bona fide magician. I every day made him a magician; it was easy to because, as the story went and still goes, he was a legendary mule whisperer. During the war he had been dutifully in charge of his battalion's mules and there'd been a particularly hard-faced mule (I think called Daisy) no one could do anything with – except for Big Jimmy Butler. Whenever this stubborn animal would stall he'd dive down into the trench, whisper into its ear, and said mule would instantly obey his command. No word of a lie here, he also sang in tongues. By that, I mean he never knew the words to any pub piano-accompanied song and would gleefully sing a surreal series of drunken yet melodic gibberish. To him, lyrics were a useless add-on, an add-on he seemingly never needed. He was a superb singer, his oddball vocal gimmick a show-stopping act 'n' incredibly popular with his pissed-up peers. There's a fantastic pub photo of him singing and looking like he just might be hangin' out with Sinatra. A searingly in-the-moment image full of rhythmic body-thumping passion and old-Joanna-accompanied verve. With his mystic mule magic, singing in drunken tongues and mysteriously never being there, it was a no-brainer to make him a powerful wizard. Being storybook crazy, I could easily turn imaginative thought into real life; I was childhood obsessed with magic, with witches, wizards and magicians. So much so, I made my long-gone, ship-scaling, unable-to-read-or-write parent one. Looking back, I now recognise it was a way of owning him.

I had several telly dads; of-the-time celebrities I'd fantasise as my father. David Nixon, the sharp-suited magician was by far the poshest of them and, like me real Da, billiard-ball-headed and full o' tricks. Dickie Henderson too, the seemingly drunken, highly-skilled, vaudevillian hoofer, always so lounge-lizardly louche 'n' elegant. He stylishly wore a jaunty-angled, half-over-the-eyes trilby, and moved like languid mercury. I adored his easy 'n' effortless tap-gliding showmanship and it was how I'd imagine Big Jimmy Butler might present himself in pubs. Then, the most sacred dad of all dads: Sid James. A hard-drinking, five-pints-in-a-one-pint-glass, horse-'n'-dogs-betting, rough-diamond, working-class archetype. Completely fitting and filling the role, he was top of the pops of my televisual bill. Sid was the padre my head would visit most; in there he took me Sunday fishing. So vivid were my paternal imaginings around Sid James, I'd make myself believe he passed on some much-needed fishing skills. Saying that though, I've never actually fished. There were occasionally others... John Wayne was an occasional dad, a one-film-only one, and I think Maureen O'Hara, a one-film-only mum (both imagined from *The Quiet Man*). My telly pas were incredibly important to me. Although living in a box in the corner of our kitchen, those flickering monochromatic arl fellas filled a role. I wasn't a bad little artist and would draw myself sat with my three telly dads, always around a long, oblong wooden table, eating and laughing.

When he wasn't a dirty, rotten, filthy, stinkin' whore-master, May would speak with deep fondness of her estranged husband: 'He was the singer and I was the dancer, Gerrid.' When she'd say that, I'd feel a panicky-fuelled frisson of love for Big Jimmy. The swishing, feathery, ballrooming idea they were somehow the Fred Astaire 'n' Ginger Rogers of spit 'n' sawdust Scottie/ Vauxy/Dock Road pubs, the sensually gliding Hollywood stars of The Honky Tonk (a popular local), filled me with unimaginable campy joy. When she wasn't shooting off fiery rages about him her voice would softly lower, almost to a whisper, proudly telling me he was a real grafter, how much the lads hero-worshipped him and, for all his skulduggering ways, a genuinely good father. Although my sense of abandonment would be horribly exacerbated by my brothers' deaths, it started long before they died with stories like these. May could freely admit she wasn't always the best mother. She was a deliberately honest woman, especially about herself, but in those tender story-telling moments she did make him sound like the best dad – even better than Sid James. There was a lot of love in May and it melancholy-sung in her voice, just speaking of him; she'd often be singing the mournful ballad of Jimmy Butler.

After Thomas's death, suddenly the world was a million-piece jigsaw of my completely puzzled family and we were carelessly hurled into a vortexing heartlessness of Hurricane Grim Rita. Although solidly held within the cold, still, brutal stasis of grief, we were literally a four-corners-scattered-everywhere mess. Emotions were no longer emotions; they'd become roaring, slavering monsters, *and how many times does a door have to be kicked or a wall punched?* Our Paul was a Kwiki bag (Scouse for 'plastic Kwik Save bag'), twisting wildly-chaotic within an (hopefully) Oz-bound tornado. Thankfully, Big John, still in possession of the surface cool of a great rocker, was amazing around all this insanity. We wouldn't have got through those months without him; his trademark stoicism and wit held us precariously together. For all his surface knockabout comedy he inwardly held a strong and powerful silence. Hard to explain, but he kind of passed it on, a bit like Nin. Of all four of us though it was our Chris breaking down most; emotionally a lot like May, except a young, handsome bloke. Ugly, bludgeoning grief forcibly tremored throughout his body, then he'd physically buckle, collapsing into sobbing tears. Also like May, he needed me, and I was good with him. All I'd do was sit, listen, and it was sometimes enough. I'm pretty sure he'd only do this with me and these are moments we'd regularly share. I must have thought *one day, when I know more words, I'll get better at it*. And did. Much better.

There were times Chris 'n' Paul poured through the door of 6A stociously (Scouse for 'pissed up') drunk, but obviously cheered up. It would be when they'd met up and been drinking with Big Jimmy Butler. It was this joy-from-grief behaviour of theirs completely cementing my idea of him being a great magician. For some magical reason (and that magical reason booze) his very presence would, like he did with his wartime mules, giddy them up. Seems he was also something of a grieving brother whisperer. It'd seldom last long, till bed at most, but to me it looked like up-tempo, joyful respite. Drunk, Chris 'n' Paul would always go on about how great he was and how one day I'd know that and him. That day never came, but it was always obvious to me he was clearly fantastic for them. When my brothers had been out getting magically healed by my wizard of a father, I still had to look after my distressed, forever-breaking-down mother. She was doing a lot more of her smothering/wailing thing, so I wanted that magical holiday away from it all too; their mystical, pub-land greatness. I desperately needed my pissed-up, joke-telling, gobbledygook-crooning dad. May never saw him after our Jimmy died. He didn't visit when Paul fell and now Thomas had gone there was still no husband, still no dad. I always thought it was me. He didn't want to see *me*. I still think that.

It's many miles wide, so expansively open you're barely a dot, it's alone and incredibly sad. More than not being wanted, more than not being seen, it's not being thought about. A drop in the ocean, but fuckin' 'ell Gerrid, look, no bleedin' ocean. You think you've put yourself here, but you haven't put yourself here, you've been put here. Feel I've always known this emptiness but here's the good part: it was my brothers' deaths finally transforming the nowhere of it all into a desert; my desert. Even if there's only you in it, at least deserts are somewhere. You can make them suddenly scenic; conjure sunshine, survive sandstorms. Sometimes there's Chinese Scouse Empresses, even Barbie dolls. Whatever it was I had to do, whyever I had to do it, I had to do it myself. And if that means imagining deserts for company then so be it.

I'd much later be told it was dissociative behaviour; I get that, but oddly, don't like the words. I know they're the right words but surely it's because of *familial association* I'm able to do this. Sometimes I'd sneak under our table and, from underneath, half-blocked-off by a tatty table cloth, I'd just watch feet. That table became a gingham-curtained stage and those fidgeting, side-to-side shifting leather-bound trotters were just being feet. Even if wearing similar shoes, no two pair were the same and, for some pantomiming reason, hysterically funny. Those signature-stepping clod-hoppers were my introduction to the avant-garde.

It's the endless storying of Scousers which makes us what we are: the great deniers. But if you can magic pictures or words, imagine funny dads, instantly fall into calming deserts or be entertained by pissed-up feet, this dissociation lark can become an incredibly useful and socially decorative tool.

Because he sung in such eloquently drunken gibberish, I know all the words to my dad's songs. He at least gave me that.

XVI
The Mersey

I've always craved aloneness, part of who and why I am. Even at eight years old it felt right to find and inhabit those *more me* spaces. Liverpool's a busy, bustling city full of the fullest, busying people; a city not only knowing the culturally-emotive importance of *alone*, but also the physicality and spirituality of isolation. For all its overcrowded busyness, there's a lot of alone in Scousers.

When escaping May, I'd skedaddle, skip and forever walk the long way around everywhere. I must've been really easily entertained because just walking through/about the local docklands and my city centre was always (and still is) more than enough entertainment. Cities aren't simply stoically bold monuments to proletariat-muscled ingenuity, they're museums, art galleries, libraries and the most creative pieces of real-lifed, immersive theatre. Every day Liverpool is different; every day everywhere is. Open eyes 'n' open heart can make anybody a visionary.

It's early Sunday evening and I'm head-bowed, round-shouldered mooching to The Pier Head. I've always thought of this particular location as the seed they planted in America to grow New York. You turn a corner and it mystically opens out, a vast expanse of concrete leading to the Mersey. The air's different here; heady, damp, ephemerally tasting of long-lived 'n' long dead remembrance. All is bare, like a desert but stony.

It'd be flat if there wasn't so much tangibly physical dimension. If any place defines the historic enormity of my city, it's the mouth of our giant river, surrounded by the majestic, architectural gestalt of The Three Graces.

I'm suddenly greeted by swirls of waving mizzle. Wet-skin weather complimenting wet eyes, and it suits my face. Grey isn't one colour; there's a lot more to it than a lifeless, silvery hue. Grey spiral-collects in mists and something about this cascading, fogging vista, instantly enlivens. From a distance, its chippy-caff and restaurant building look like a cubist mirage fading into the rippling, slate-sheen, glide of river. Over the water, Cammell Laird's shipyard's a far-off dimly-lit-mythical, and New Brighton's doing a fantastic impersonation of us. Very few figures populate, some of them standing, some sitting alone. They first appear as school-pencil drawings you've rubbed out but, like phantom images after erasure, there's still a slight suggestion of them left behind. Because I now know death, it doesn't bother me everybody looks like ghosts.

I sit on a bench with two cigarette-smoking old blokes. They're wrinkly-lined, relief-map skinned and head-to-toe covered in cap, scarf 'n' overcoat, finished off in big-leathered boot. They immediately say things, funny things and, all the time looking to the Mersey, ask if I'm alright. Also looking to the Mersey, I say, 'Yeah.' There's a hypnotic grab to this river, never letting you go. In many ways you are it. The mesmerising quality it clearly possesses immediately chills you out. You're not perfectly relaxed, that's not what she does; she lavishly bestows upon you the space to mull difficult things with ease. The Mersey's a generous narcissist too, and she knows it. She's who we get it off.

In summer months The Pier Head's completely different, its grass verges full of noisily enlivened families. On blistering hot Sunday afternoons, with a bag packed with sugar butties and bottles of lemo, Mary Mac would take Little John, Stephen and

I on a great day out. Winter though, with a slowly enveloping dusk and boozy old men talking of sailing the seven seas, it clairvoyant-like channels a vast inhabitable mausoleum. A perfectly pleasant mausoleum mind, with clearly alive, jangling Scousers.

A lot of invisible information hovers around The Pier Head and its river. A nautical but nice sing-song intonation genteelly whistles through its always-humming atmosphere, melodically adding to the auld sung, sea-salty Blues of these scrappily chatting ex-sailors. They're adding their gravelling up-tempo voices to it; a circular song, particularly in this mizzling greyness of which everybody's a part. I'm not sure what they're actually singing but it doesn't matter. The elemental choir of new and long dead Scousers chorally haunting us won't let them get a word in edgewise; even deathly quiet this city won't shut up.

There are chains clanking, old timbers creaking, and every half hour big burly boats smash into huge rubber tyres, mightily delivering delightfully crashing, time-honouring thuds. Long before those four lads it was our ferries giving Liverpool (therefore the world) a good shake.

It's getting quite dark. Big sky, bored by this every-night choir of ghosts, is black-cloud-grumbling and the two blokes, concerned, tell me it's high time to get home. I think they know I'm out of sorts and, even through their laughter, I know they are. I don't know exactly why, but they are. Whatever's been said, what's left unspoken, can say more than words. All three of us silently know staring at the sea is listening in to *other* conversation. One of them gives me a thru'penny bit and tells to get some sweets. I gladly take it, say thanks, and his comedic, funny-voiced shooing-away-of-me's so friendly, I smile.

Sometimes asked if I've ever had imaginary friends. I've always said no, but I'm lying through my back teeth. The Pier Head's full of them.

XVII
The Death of Blackstock Gardens

Blackstock Gardens is dying.

Can't exactly pinpoint when first noticing, but feels like closing your eyes in one time then *abracadabra alakazam!* its sixteen weeks later and you're opening them in another. People have been moving out for some months; every day I see a removal lorry or cart being loaded, sometimes several, and neighbours, people I've known all my young life, driven or pulled away. I think it a depressing sight anyway but, after all we've been through, everything over our landing suddenly appears a slow 'n' trundling funereal. What was once a dream housing complex for so many hovel-dwelling Scousers now a city-council-declared, soon-to-be-demolished slum. All is dimming, mournfully romantically, but also in clear-as-day reality. At night, our lengthy landings usually window-glimmered with soft-lit, curtains-drawn amber or sometimes a gaudy, pink-nets glare. Now there are long lengths of shadow with only the occasional glowing, translucent portal. These dooming corridor stretches of darkness separating still-lit flats look like the black light of grief.

Because of everybody being moved out it all gradually becomes quieter, as if the tenement itself is silencing. The landing's nightly-chorused, inebriate singing, gradually winding down. I've long thought I knew where we lived that little bit more than anybody else; being bezzies, our tenement and I are on first name terms. It's always *Blackie* to me and I'm damn well sure it calls me Gerrid/Jelly Beans; the chimneys deffo do. It's sad Blackie, and knows there are a lot less of us playing Rush. I know it knows; we're nowhere near as beautifully noisy. People are the lifeforce of any successful cohabitation, but it's also the buildings: it's this behemoth of an edifice housing so many colourful histories, lively characters, big families and mad kids. Whatever the adventure, whatever the party, whatever the hilarity or sadness, all our stories held together by the red brick, gaping-arched, wide-open magnanimity of Blackstock Gardens. How can they so easily, so swiftly, knock down these noble Scouse castles and why disperse this decades-long, interconnected community? People are angry with the insulting descriptor of *slum* being insensitively bandied about. It genuinely upsets everybody, especially the women. Those fiercely warrior, house-proud, Windowlene-, Brasso-, Vim-, Omo-brandishing Valkyries are seriously pissed off. Saying that, some people get really big posh council houses with two gardens, and saying that, some don't. Even after all that has happened, my family and I don't want to say goodbye. In a silently messaging way, because of this turgid hollowing-out, it's gradually saying goodbye to us.

Me Ma couldn't leave the house without having a nervous breakdown, so talk of moving all we had to somewhere else would have further freaked her out. I still can't properly picture my mother, nearly all my memories of her at this time being completely blocked. I remember Annie King taking me to one side, telling me no one had been through what May had been through, that she was remarkable and I should look after her. Whilst I always believed Annie, me Ma didn't seem too remarkable to me. In truth, I'm not completely sure she was anything. May would later tell me she was gone and gone for a long time, perhaps so gone she'd kinda disappeared. Whatever or wherever May was now, she wasn't a fully-functioning mother; that became my job. I'd had to stay in 6A with her a lot more often, but sitting with her when she clearly wasn't in the same room upset me. With the deaths of my two brothers, near deaths of three, and non-manifestations of my ersatz-magical dad, when sat with her I'd sorta go too. It's funny how someone not being there haunts. Big Jimmy Butler was ghost dad, May his ghost wife, and I his ghost kid. Everything and everybody was ghosting. I wonder if I told Annie what I'd promised me Nin?

Even though the Gardens were emptying, the factories, pubs, churches, boxing clubs around were still up 'n' running. Outside the creaking Castle Frankenstein of our flat there was an eclectically alive, ongoing world. Liverpudlians are by 'n' large a gregariously enlivened peoples; even when raging they're more often than not laughing at raging. Mary Mac was superb at being able to laugh at her own temper. Yup, a commonplace platitude, but there'll be a gnawing worm of truth wriggling its way through every cliché. Scousers have an innate way of negotiating the armour and intellect of humour. It's in the irreverent blood, bones 'n' flesh of our never-ending storytelling. Travelling the streets on my own, walking my secret ways to our city centre, I could physically see that naturally light-hearted ebullience. Often looking like dancing, it continually cheered me. I'm not in any way saying Scousers didn't live in abject poverty, didn't have hard lives or weren't horrible, sometimes violent people, home alone drunks or awful, abusive parents, of course some of them were 'n' still are, but visually there was always something characterfully *extra* about them. I clearly see it convivially similar in Belfast 'n' Glasgow.

When on my Scottie/Vauxhall/Dock Road travels, I'd get to really know the women in shops, especially stores like bakeries or chandlers (Scouse for Aladdin's Cave-like 'hardware shop'). Seeing you by yourself, they'd look out for you more; make sure they knew your name and were forever giving out sweets. Walking past pubs, old blokes stood outside mysteriously seemed to know you. These beetroot-cheeked sots can't possibly recognise who you are, but that doesn't in any way stop them thinking they can. With a noise resembling a half-death-rattle mixed in with a scathing chuckle, they'd gummy-spit out an unintelligible joke. I'd've met these ancient galleons, these drunken junks for little less than five minutes and before I knew it be waving a fond farewell to them like they're a long-lost granddad. Chippy's would green-sheen welcome and, in the queue waiting for a bag of chips, a lightly battered sausage and a carton of curry, would be that same hit of humorous bantering. Again, a rasping-dry, knowingly sly-eyed, wry-smiling delivery, almost always ending in an atmosphere-crackling sixty-a-day cackle. I write a lot of poetry about Liverpool and am often asked why. I always reply because it's easy to. In romantic blasts of chosen memory, in search of surreal, lyrical imagery for in-the-moment living, for the fall-outing audacities of hilarity and tragedy, Liverpool *is* a poem.

I remember the Liverpool of my early childhood far more happily before my brother's deaths. It would be some time after I'd start remembering it positively again. It's why I often talk/write of a near-full employed, high-waged, low rent, municipally-engined sixties. Although we emerged from quite definite poverty, we finally got out of that poverty. I was also a child with a much fuller, happier family, and it largely, socially, communally worked for me. There are sepia-led halcyon tinges you can't help but fall into – more than that, *want* to fall into. Today, you can't go into any Liverpool pub that's home to an older crowd without conversations turning to the sixties; conversations of many colours, high-energy jangle of the tenements, of fondly remembered neighbours and of partying, pub-enthused laughter. It's not just nostalgia; it's passionate/compassionate, emotively-driven communication. I believe that after the two big wars, and especially come the sixties, the working class somehow knew they'd built 'n' rebuilt the world twice (most Scousers will boastfully tell you they've sailed around it). Being so hands-on vital to all this collectively necessary, brand new world-building was all part of their bourgeoning confidence. Everyone in Cons 'n' Gerrys instinctively/professionally knew they were an important part of a wider, societal, even global conversation.

What's left to say when after all that hard work, that essential resorting 'n' restructuring, you're forcibly taken out of said conversation? Wanting or needing to remember the city-aggrandising enormities of all you were, of what you were empowered by, isn't blandly chowing down on regurgitated, rose-tinted nostalgia. It's present day survival. It seriously pisses me off when people carelessly diss nostalgia; I think it class-biased, unintellectually informed, social erasure. Confidently reanimating when you were integrally part of something, even if romancing and embellishing said something, is more than just another funny story about Annie King. It's keeping dynamic working-class peoples, their histories, joys, defeats and achievements orally alive. Memories were people too y'know! My head's full of human event, a Technicolor, monochromatic, kaleidoscopic spiral of people/places, constantly tumbling and forever reshaping.

...She's called Miss Purcell. Big red hair, dramatic purple dress and seemingly forever haloed by an arc of choraling daffodils. It's one of my first days at St. Brigid's infant school and we're all in our vests, underpants 'n' knickers, barefoot on the criss-cross certainties of parquet. It feels great underfoot, like a wooden floor should, like it never would again. There's a just-polished, pine-like scent and spring light pours through huge black-framed windows; brightness bathes our pasty skins. I'm instantly entranced by the bendy collisions of our floor shadows; we look like a dark, malleable crowd of sprites. A seemingly gliding Miss Purcell diaphanously wafts to the end of the hall, operatically approaching a huge, oval-shaped, wooden object with a dark, round, metal grill. She turns a big, black Bakelite dial, there's an ears-cussing, hissing squall and, as if by magic, the most melodically enchanting music fills everywhere. Suddenly everything is an airy other-worldly; the tiny motes of dust we're kicking up in the sunshine look like miniscule fairies. I don't hear if she asks us to freely dance, but Miss Purcell's voice is so full of flowing Isadora Duncan-esque movement we just do…

…On Vauxhall Road, not far from the mock-Tudor elegance of Eldon Grove, next door to Portland Gardens, is The Simmy. No idea what *Simmy* is short for, but it's a railings-surrounded park space with swings, a huge roundabout and monkey bars. Because it's always chained-up, padlock-locked, we can't get in through its wrought iron front gate. But two of its railings have been jemmied apart to make sure we always have access; I am forever wondering if our Tommy has pulled them open. Simple and roughshod as it is, The Simmy's our own private Disney-land where we after-school play, often till dusk. Every other tenement is in there with us, but it always feels *ours*. Love the jagged scrape of the Corporation green-chipped paint on the bent bars we squeeze through. Scrunching tight our tiny ribs, it always catches, snags at and sometimes tiny-rips our clothes…

…It's winter outside St. Brigid's. The afternoon has welcomed an almighty blizzard and I'm on my way home. Walking, I stumble into a huge bank of freezing snow, so massive it over-my-head engulfs. I immediately panic, am screaming for help, when I'm picked up by a wide-faced, middle-aged man with jet black hair. Gently calming me down, he introduces himself as Ray and asks where I live. I tell him and he takes me in his car to 6A. On our way he's forever reassuring and telling me jokes. Knocking on our door, a visibly concerned May opens it and Ray tells her what's happened to me. 'Take no notice mister,' says me Ma, 'he's always cryin'.' Before she can hurriedly shut the door, Ray passes her a bar of chocolate and a toy. It's a battered brown monkey. The same monkey our Tommy will use over our kitchen door as a terrifying puppet. As the front door shuts, May immediately smacks the back of my head, 'What have I told ye Gerrid about gettin' into cars with strange men? He could 'ave done anything to ye. Oh, yi'v already got me 'arrished (Scouse for 'panicked') today lad. I'll 'ave to sit down, me fuckin' nerves are shot 'ere!' I take the scraggy monkey and delicious chocolate from a clearly 'arrished May and think black-haired Ray lovely; for a while, an imaginary dad…

…Does every area in Liverpool have its own Nickynackynoona? Is there a whooping, manic gang of rictus-grinning Nicky-nackynoonas? Or is it this same Nickynackynoona ghost-riding around all of Merseyside on his bike, clearly off his rocker, whirling a chain wildly above his head, screaming out his name, scaring the livin' bejebers out of us and, with hacking, Nickynackynoona-like-glee, chasing us petrified kids around our square? We're panicky screeching scram, fearing for our very lives and bombing it to our parts of the stairwells to escape. From the high up safety of the landings, we laughingly yell his impossible name back at him and love it. No sooner has Nickynackynoona tried to cold-bloodily murder us, off he zooms to whatever fiery hell dimension he emerged from. He's got to be related to Spring Heeled Jack…

…For some reason I can't recall, perhaps because of my lack lustre school attendance, I make my first confession and first Holy Communion one year later than I should. May is unable to take me so I'm accompanied by Mary Mac. I'm beyond thrilled at the chunky woollen-knit of my wooden-buttoned, almost-golden-looking Communion cardigan. I've a dickie-bow that I'm over-the-moon made-up with, brown sandal-like shoes and grey shorts. I go to the altar and take the Body of Christ. With Jesus slowly dissolving on my tongue (he's a sour-tasting chalky) and like I'm walking on air, I make my way back to our Mary. I've a Bible, a Rosary, and my hands are clasped together in prayer mode. Side-shifting my body through the pew, I sit alongside her. Looking down, she winks, elbows my shoulder, and tells me I looked the best...

...A friend of me Ma's, Joan, has a daughter with a serious health problem: a hole in her heart. Joan tells my mother that her daughter must undergo tricky, lifesaving surgery and that she'll throw a massive street party for all the kids in Blackstock Gardens if her daughter pulls through. The daughter does pull through and Joan dutifully keeps her promise – and what a fantastic do it is. There'd certainly been other street parties, but because we are celebrating the survival of Joan's daughter, one of our own, there's a special merrying high-kick to this particular shindig. Spread all over our big square, surrounded by non-stop jangling mothers, tables overflow with sweets, crisps, lemonade 'n' jelly. Every family does their bit. I recognise some of our neighbours' furniture; on the street it looks odd, like it's been magicked there. Under the table, by my leg, she's expectantly panting; I pass Queenie the Alsatian the slices of boiled ham I've slyly liberated from their cobs (Scouse for 'bap'). The whole party ends in a giant game of manically-enthused, sugared-up Rush...

...St. Patrick's Day always feels a little daytime weighty, like the air itself has changed. Not sad weighty, more instinctively reverent and silently acknowledged. A simple floral decoration gives the game away; on most people's lapels, tin-foil-wrapped sprigs of cascading shamrock. This slightly sonorous tone is about so many families remembering, honouring their first/ second/third generation Irishness, but that weight's soon lifted as the pubs come alive. There is always singing to be heard in our locals but, whatever the song, it is powerfully and more passionately sung on St. Pat's. This is also an excellent evening to hang outside those pubs to once again pick up the odd thru'penny bit or sixpence thrown at us. After the pubs have closed our landings are never more alive with longingly, lovelorn, heartfelt singing…

…I walk into Marshall's paper shop and Mary Mac's eyes reach to high heaven, 'Oh dear God, what d'you want and make it quick.' I don't make it quick and have Mary tutting my every choice. 'Fuckin 'ell Gerrid, I've got other customers 'ere, 'urry it up will ye!' Then I see it, shining out at me, the *TV Times* and, on its cover, Diana Rigg. I'm immediately overjoyed, instantly buy it and, to our Mary's obvious delight, speedily leave. I've bought comics many times before but this is my first ever grown-up magazine and in it four whole pages dedicated to my favourite Avenger. I sit on the steps of what's shaped like a li'l turret and it genuinely feels like Blackstock Gardens is leaning over my shoulder to read with me. Normally I'd shoo away anyone peering over me to blimp what I'm comic-book devouring, but Blackie always gets a get out of jail free card. There are so many photos of Diana, lots as Mrs Peel, and I'm in kinky, cat-suited, Avengers heaven. Then I read it, her birth date, making my jaw drop into the centrefold staples. Diana Rigg, my favourite televisual human being, my role model hero, my sat-behind-my-mother-weekly-inspiration and I share the same birthday: July 20th. I scream in out-loud effeminate joy and, no word of a lie, tell the tenement the news. No word of a lie, Blackie's thrilled too. I'm gonna have to tell Susan Graham we're no longer twins and that she, Emma Peel and I, are indeed triplets…

…At an urgent pace our Janet walks into 6A, in her hand a rolled-up magazine, probably that week's *The Weekend*. She looks a keen wide-eyed different, like she knows something important. May asks, 'What's up girl, nottin' bad is it?' Janet tells May that there's an article in the magazine maybe explaining why she can't leave the house. Me Ma, immediately interested, eagerly takes it from Janet's hands. An intense, instant silence swallows the kitchen and it's as if we're all somehow hearing something unravelling. May, riveted to the article, eventually looks up. Visibly moved, she says, 'That's it girl, exactly it, aggaphobia, this is what I've got.' For the pulp magazine it was, it was a quite detailed piece on agoraphobia and the first time any of us had read or said the word wrong (it took May a little while 'n' practise to be able to properly pronounce it). After my brothers died, this is one of the few good memories I have of my mother. For a little while she snapped out of her grief, her face showing a contentment-like joy about knowing the name of what had for four years been plaguing her. She was properly smiling. There was a brief suggestion of confidence; she'd finally learnt something about herself and her complexing condition, and for the first time in a long, long time, she was in the room. Remember our Janet saying, 'No word of a lie May, I've just this minute said to our Kathleen, I'm gonna fly over to 6A right now an' show 'er, cos this 'as got May Butler written all over it.'…

…In a giant cardboard box nicked from the BXL, before bravely going into battle, my wife Sharon Flood kisses me on the cheek. My very first kiss. The Second World War still features heavily; we're forever being told all about it and many times play at going to war. Blackstock Gardens was hit very badly in the 1940 December Blitz. Being so near the docks made it, by seafaring association, one of Mr Hitler's prime targets (there's a picture of it after the bombing and it's an epic mess of rubbled devastation). The Blackstock Gardens air raid shelter built on our big square took a direct hit, killing two hundred people, including four of the then residents of 6A: Elizabeth Janet Clarke, John Clarke, Mary Clarke, William Clarke; I just want to mention their names. There are many long, drawn out, whispered stories of the war, The Liverpool Blitz, and the ghosts of Blackstock Gardens. When it comes to stories for Duck Apple Night, we have a neighbourly plethora of tragic spooks to choose from. May was forever telling us we were playing on the graves of our people.

We had been offered one of those big council houses with two gardens in Noggzy (Scouse for 'Norris Green', a somewhat greener area of Liverpool, miles away from town). There was some talk about it and for a little while I thought that was where we were going to move to. Although I love grass, flowers and trees, don't think I want to move away from all of this. I'm used to the city centre, massive factories, the Dock Road; adore playing around huge ships and rust riddled, creaking industry.

In my splattered flashes of memory there's an all-pervading sense of something being over. Of course, it's familial grief, but there's far more to it than that. The red brick bouquets are wilting. Watching so many people saying goodbye is odd and upsetting (to this day I'm not very good at it). It feels enormously adult, with back-slapping 'n' hugs all round. Big John's face in particular forever housing a resigned, half-smiled sadness, his eyes deadened by farewells. Because of so many fires being built on so many 'ollers, the air is its usual burnt-misting, allowing what electric lights still lit to become even more soul-shaped. There are times I can touch the air and almost feel someone or something's there, but they're not; where do all these memories, these energies go?

But we're not moving to Noggzy. May's had an offer to move to the same street as her mother. I'm going to be near my magical Nin. A part of me is overjoyed by that, but we none of us want to leave Blackie.

A spitting-with-rain late-November evening and from our landing I see the removal lorry arrive. Like a long, bare hearse, it parks below our landing. The lads immediately start loading the glum-looking truck with what little we possess and have rope-wrapped our tiny world in green-sheeted tarpaulin. All we own now looks like a big, baggy, rained-on, ugly parcel. One you might not want to open. There's Big John, Mary Mac, Little John, Stephen and new baby nephew, Paul. Little John, Stephen and I are messing about on the landing and from below I hear our Paul shout, 'C'mon Gerrid, get down 'ere now, time to go kid.' I don't want to go but I'm a kid and have to.

Lit by the vehicle's headlights, Big John's face reveals his heart 'n' soul. Inside the lorry I'm sat on our Chris's knee. What little's left of our community waves us off and we wave back. I enjoy the nose-clammy, oil-pungent hit of being inside the cabin... until it turns the corner onto Vauxhall Road. In unison, we look back and without words all say goodbye to Blackie.

High above, brave and guarding, he suddenly appears: the sword-'n'-shield-baring Mr Cube, the giant emblem of Tate & Lyle sugar refiners. We'd often play underneath him; he felt mythically protecting and I'm pretty sure nightly saw off Spring Heeled Jack (perhaps even Nickynackynoona). But this toweringly enormous, blue-flickering neon warrior soon gets smaller 'n' smaller 'n' smaller.

To this day I can still feel Blackstock Gardens being slowly taken from me. 6A would be no more and Blackstock Gardens itself would soon be demolished.

Demolished, what an ugly word.

It takes very few minutes to get to our new home: the top floor of a pedestrian-looking, only three-high block of flats. It's immediately drab and uninviting. I instinctively know I won't ever play Rush or Two-balls again... and never be truly happy at 7B Lapworth Street.

She Laments in Whisper
for May Butler

Sitting with and drowning in story,
no word un-meant, no song un-sung.
In comfort of armchair and coming up for air,
she queen'd, Sheba'd.

Talked of dancing like it was semaphore,
weaving through her lips and hands.
Had no idea the storyteller she was,
because until I told her, no one told her
and when I told her,
she cried.

Spoke in pictures, like poets should,
like sometimes they don't.
Told her she was a poet.
Told me, no one had told her anything,
no one complimented, no one took time.
Apparently in the past,
it was embarrassing to compliment.
She'd a way of looking beyond and into,
as much window as son.

When tea cauldrons, silence spells
and incantation waits its turn.
All her life, her losses and finds.
Wiser than tree, earth and wave.
Every exquisitely carved letter of her story.

#6ablackstockgardens
flapjackpress.co.uk